Behavior with a Purpose

by
Richard Delaney, PhD.
and
Charley Joyce, LICSW

Better Endings New Beginnings

Behavior with a Purpose

Copyright © 2009
Richard Delaney, Charley Joyce

Published by:
Better Endings New Beginnings
www.betterendings.org

Printed in United States of America

If you purchase this book without a cover you should be aware that this book may be stolen property and reported as "unsold or destroyed" to the publisher. In such case, neither the author nor the publisher has received any payment for this stripped book.

All Rights Reserved. Except as permitted under U.S. Copyright Act of 1976, no part of this publication may be reproduced, stored in a retrieval system, or transmitted by any means - electronic, mechanical, photocopying, recording or otherwise - without written permission from the publisher.

ISBN 978-0-9842007-4-0
Library of Congress Control Number 2009937530

*Dedicated to:
AFK (Adoptive, Foster, Kinship)
youth and their caregivers*

"As an adoptive parent of children
from foster care, I am always
looking for relevant parenting books.
'Behavior with a Purpose'
offers me answers to many of those
'Why does he DO that?'
questions that I ask.
Thank you for offering
AFK parents this great reference!"

Deb Fjeld

Acknowledgements

*As a social worker and a psychologist
we are a "work in progress" as writers.*

*As a result, we are deeply appreciative of
Deb Fjeld, Jodee Kulp, Karl Kulp Jr. and Gretchen Joyce
for their incredibly patient, ongoing editing of
Behavior with a Purpose.*

Thank you.

Authors' Notes

The majority of the case examples in the book are factual or composites of several children's experiences to illustrate a specific behavioral problem. Case examples are used to make "Behavior with a Purpose" real for the reader. Names and other identifying factors have been changed in each example to preserve confidentiality. Unfortunately, we have been unable to list and credit many AFK (Adoptive, Foster, or Kinship) parents, child welfare workers, and therapists as this would jeopardize the confidentiality of the youth they have served.

Each chapter had a primary author so you will note that there are writing style differences and slight structural differences within the book. We hope that these slight variations will enhance learning rather than cause any distractions.

We truly treasure the opportunities that AFK youth, parents, and child welfare workers have provided for us to learn from them and to be a part of their lives. We hope that we have served them well in our own helping efforts and also through the contents of this book. It is our ultimate hope that "Behavior with a Purpose," will help the reader understand the point and purpose of behavior problems, and how to positively influence behaviors impacted by abuse, neglect, and separation, loss and multiple moves.

Richard Delaney, PhD and Charley Joyce, LICSW

Contents

- 5 **Preface**
  - 5 Typical Behavior Problems of Foster, Kinship, Adopted Children
  - 8 How Do We Get to the Bottom of Why Children and Youth Act Out?
  - 9 Sizing Up the Structure of a Behavior Problem
  - 12 Testing Out Hypothesis Once We Have a Hunch about Why a Child Has a Behavior Problem?
  - 13 A Brief Look at Our Underlying Principles
  - 15 A Sneak Preview of Each Chapter

- 18 **Chapter 1.**
  Introduction: The Collision Between the AFK Child and the AFK Family
  - 18 Wanting to Serve
  - 19 Bob and Shirley Take-Up the Call to Serve
  - 20 Matt's Unstable Stability
  - 25 Angela Doesn't Like Formal Introductions
  - 28 Why Collisions Take Place

- 34 **Chapter 2.**
  Hoarding Food; Hungry for Security
  - 35 How Does Neglect Impact Hoarding
  - 36 Case in Point: Patti
  - 44 Differential Diagnosis
  - 49 Final Remarks

50 **Chapter 3.**
Wetting Behavior; when it Rains, it Pours
    51   Case in Point: Carrie, Protective/Anxiety Wetting
    56   Case in Point: Jenna, Anger/Control Wetting
    60   Case in Point: Joey, Wetting that is Reminiscent of Home
    64   Case in Point: Darwin, Wetting as a Symptom of Neglect
    66   Assessment Factors
    68   Differential Diagnosis
    71   Final Remarks

72 **Chapter 4.**
Lying and Stealing
    74   Case in Point: Barbie, Stealing
    81   Case in Point: J.T., Lying
    83   Figuring Out How Lying and Deception Work for the Child
    87   Differential Diagnosis
    89   Final Remarks

91 **Chapter 5.**
Defiance May Not be What it Appears to be
    93   Case in Point: Gretchen, Anxious Defiance
    102   Case in Point: Jenny, Angry Defiance
    107   Case in Point: Robert, Patterned Defiance
    111   Case in Point: Morgan, Defiance of a Self-Parented Child
    115   Differential Diagnosis
    117   Final Remarks

118 **Chapter 6.**
Naughty, Naughty: Relentless Negative Behaviors
- 120 Case in Point: Carson, Negative Attention-Seeking Behavior
- 127 Differential Diagnosis
- 128 Final Remarks

129 **Chapter 7.**
The Wisdom of the Experts,
What AFK Youth and AFK Families Have Taught Us
- 130 Protecting Myself from Potentially Hurtful Adults
- 132 I Want to be with People That Look like Me
- 134 Blood is Thick and Forever
- 137 Kodak Moments Mean People Care About Me
- 140 I Don't Have a Sleep Disorder; I Just Want to Feel Safe
- 141 I Need to Center Myself Before I Start the Day
- 143 I Need to Feel Comfortable in Order to Shower
- 145 I'll Fight so I Can Know My Father
- 146 I Need Distance From My Feelings
- 148 Help Me Self-Soothe in a Non-sexual Way

151 Conclusion
153 About the Authors
155 Index

Preface

"Typically, there are multiple causes for problem behaviors that require diverse methods of identification."[1]

Typical Behavior Problems of Foster, Kinship and Adopted Children

It may come as no surprise to helping professionals who work with foster, kinship and adopted children that as many as three out of four foster children and youth suffer from serious mental health problems. [2] Many of these same children have three or more psychiatric disorders. [3]

The most common diagnoses include:
- Reactive attachment disorder
- Rost traumatic stress disorder
- Bi-polar disorder
- Attention deficit hyperactivity disorder
- Oppositional defiant disorder
- Conduct disorder
- Autistic spectrum disorders

---

1 Cone, 1997; Flannery et al., 1995; Hayes and O'Brien, 1990

2 Simms, Dubowitz, & Szilagyi, 2000

3 Iwata, et al., 1982

The number of diagnoses AFK (Adoptive, Foster, or Kinship) children carry seems to be positively correlated to the number of mental health professionals who have seen them. Over time they become, as one foster parent aptly put it, "the alphabet soup kids." Often, there is an on-going dispute over which of the array of assigned diagnoses is most accurate. While the debate continues, AFK parents are left to contend with their youngster's symptoms, which often is a bewildering assortment of behavioral and emotional issues.

Our work with foster, kinship, and adoptive parents (and their children and youth) confirms what studies have shown; many of their children struggle mightily with emotional and behavioral problems. And, to be candid, AFK parents struggle to help their children. Many of these children show conduct problems which will not go away. These problems commonly include both externalizing and internalizing behavioral problems such as lying, stealing, hoarding food, anger outbursts, self-harm, sexualized behavior, bedwetting, and defiance.

As you might already know, these behaviors often relate to critical factors such as genetic predispositions, prenatal exposure to drugs and/or alcohol, maltreatment, and multiple moves in foster care. Looking at only one of these critical factors, e.g., child neglect, the Children's Bureau summarized a long list of associated behavioral problems (see Table 1). These include such things as low self-esteem, difficulty accepting affection, fighting, delinquent behavior, drug and alcohol abuse, self-harm, withdrawal, sleep problems, or poor coping skills.

Table 1
Behavioral Problems of Neglected Children[4]

Neglected children, even when older, may display a variety of emotional and behavioral problems, including:

- Inability to control emotions, impulses, or temper outbursts
- Submissiveness
- Learning difficulties in school and problems with siblings or classmates
- Unusual eating or sleeping behaviors
- Fighting or soliciting sexual interactions
- Soliciting sexual interactions
- Social or emotional immaturity
- Unresponsiveness to affection
- Apathy or lethargy
- Lack of flexibility, persistence, or enthusiasm
- Helplessness under stress
- Poor coping skills
- Acting highly dependent
- Self-abusive behavior (e.g., suicide attempts or cutting themselves)
- Dissociative disorders, attention-deficit/hyperactivity disorder, or post-traumatic stress disorder
- Depression, anxiety, or low self-esteem
- Engaging in sexual activities leading to teen pregnancy or fatherhood
- Low academic achievement
- Alcohol or drug abuse

---

[4] http://www.acf.hhs.gov/programs/cb/stats_research/index.htm

How Do We Get
To The Bottom Of Why
Children and Youth Act Out?

It's a given that AFK children and youth often suffer from significant emotional and behavioral problems.

*How can parents and professionals
help these kids?
How can we help them end their
behavior problems?*

In short, help begins with a thorough assessment (medical, psychiatric, psychological, educational, etc.) aimed at understanding the child. An assessment also needs to uncover why the behavior problems exist and/or persist. To accomplish this, parents and professionals may need to read between the lines and decode behavior for its underlying meaning. But, how can we as parents and professionals do that? Simply put, it helps to use a two step process; first, look at *what* is happening, and then ask *why* it is happening.

Step One:
Look at What is Happening

The first step zeroes in on exactly what is happening. The emphasis here is to observe the surface behavior and its structure. We ask; What does the problem consist of? How does it look to us? At this point we also consider whether the supposed problem is normal or abnormal.

Routinely, we size up the behavior problem more precisely by asking some fairly standard questions which are, in shorthand form, what, when, where, how often, and with whom? That is, what does the problem behavior consist of? When does the problem behavior occur? When does it happen? How frequently? With whom does the problem behavior occur?

Table 2 lists the questions and some sample answers related to a child who has a problem with lying.

Table 2 Sizing Up The Structure Of A Behavior Problem	
Problem behavior:	**Lying**
What?	Child tells lies.
When?	Whenever he is asked a question.
How often?	All the time.
Where?	Mostly at school.
With Whom?	Mostly with men.

Step Two:
Look Into Why it is Happening

The second step is an examination of why the behavior problem is happening. Specifically, after pinpointing the structure of the problem, we collect information on function. *

* Note: problem behavior typically serves some function—purpose, reason, cause, meaning, or motive—or functions for the individual. That is, it serves the child or youth in some fashion. Sometimes a specific behavior problem can serve several different functions at once or over time. Alternatively, several behavior problems can serve a single function.

As mentioned earlier, function encompasses the reasons for, causes of, and purpose behind the behavior problem. In a nutshell, an examination of function focuses on finding what lies beneath the surface behavior. We look at what produces it, what maintains it, and, critically, how it serves the child. Sometimes there is a single, solitary function that a behavior problem serves. At other times, there are multiple functions associated with the behavior problem. Importantly, we don't always know exactly why a behavior problem occurs. Our examination of function really amounts to generating a working hypothesis, a helpful hunch about why the problem exists. Testing the hypothesis comes later.

Here are nine common functions we find useful in our assessment of why behavior problems may occur.

1. **ATTENTION:** A youth gains and maintains attention, sometimes "negative attention," from interactions with others. *Example: A child lies and receives a cross examination. He doesn't mind being cross examined because it is a form of attention, albeit negative attention.*

2. **ASKING FOR A NEED/WANT TO BE MET:** A youth may be communicating a need or want, though some-

times in a roundabout way. *Example: He wants to watch television, so he claims to have no homework.*

3. **FEAR OR PHOBIA:** A youth may have an automatic and powerful response to certain triggers or situations. *Example: A child is afraid of being abused if he confesses the truth.*

4. **AVOIDING OR ESCAPING:** A youth's behavior may serve to help avoid or escape some undesirable, unpleasant event, task or individual. *Example: A child blames another child for an infraction he committed, attempting to escape consequences.*

5. **REDUCE ANXIETY/PAIN:** May reduce tension or discomfort that a youth feels. *Example: Homework makes him feel stupid in the evening like he feels stupid all day long at school. He claims to have no homework to reduce his feelings of humiliation and failure.*

6. **PROVIDE STIMULATION/PLEASURE:** Behaviors may be fundamentally rewarding and pleasurable. *Example: A child derives some satisfaction from fooling adults. After telling a convincing lie, he can observe and enjoy his family's gullibility.*

7. **FAMILY ISSUES:** Issues or changes in the family may result in certain behavior and behavior problems in a youth. *Example: The arrival of a new foster child in the home occasions an increase in lying by the child already in the home.*

8. **PHYSICAL/MEDICAL:** physical ailments and psychiatric/neurological disorders can produce certain problem behaviors or symptoms. Significant attention should be placed on the connection between behaviors and fetal alcohol spectrum disorders (FASD) if alcohol usage during pregnancy is suspected or known. (For practical ideas of working with children with FASDs visit www.toolboxparent.com.} *Example: A youth with ADHD lies to cover up poor decisions and impulsive behavior. He may impulsively steal something without prior thought to consequences. When confronted, he lies to conceal his impulsive theft.*

9. **COGNITIVE DISTORTION:** some behaviors naturally spring from distortions in a youth's thinking or from irrational thoughts. *Example: A youth's early experiences have caused him to conclude that it's better (read: safer) to conceal the truth from adults.*[5]

Step Three:
Testing Our Hypothesis Once We Have A Hunch About Why A Child Has A Behavior Problem

We need to develop a strategy or approach to help the child. Once we have developed a working hypothesis or hunch about why a child acts the way he does, we can develop interventions to address the function, purpose, reason

---

5 [From Horner, R.H., Carr, E.G. (1997). Behavioral support for students with severe disabilities: Functional assessment and comprehensive intervention. Journal of Special Education, 31, 84-104).

or cause. By accurately identifying the reasons behind a behavior, interventions will be more tailored, effective, and more appropriate.[6] It also permits us to help the child adopt a "replacement behavior," or a "functionally equivalent behavior," that addresses the underlying function in a way that satisfies the child, and is acceptable to the parent. Accurate identification of the complicated and sometimes transient functions or causes of behavior demands gathering information from a variety of sources, using a variety of perspectives. From there, understanding the functions of behavior can lead to one or sometimes several simultaneous helping interventions.

A Brief Look at Our Underlying Principles

Here are some principles or assumptions underlying our work with AFK children, youth, and their families.

1. **It is essential to look beyond the obvious.**
   The surface behavior, or what is easy to see, is not an endpoint, but a beginning. We need to go deeper. (Look at the nine reasons outlined above.) This doesn't demand wallowing in murky, mumbo-jumbo that is divorced from anything we can witness or collect information on. We can benefit from an understanding of what impinges on the child; what tips the balance towards misbehavior, what may account for behaviors which appear to be unneeded, out-of-con-

---

6 Iwata, et al., 1982

text, and flatly strange at the present time. The child's history can be mined for function, with valuable nuggets of explanation.

2. **Behavior problems can be seen as opportunities.** It's important never to waste a crisis. Beyond the obvious behavior problems we'd like to get rid of are meanings and messages that the child is ill-equipped to express in other ways. We will find that it is much more productive to see children's behavior not as pathological, but as functional (given their history and their view of us and themselves.) In fact, much bad behavior is bad in the "now," but, was life saving in the past. Returning to the example of lying behavior, we need to develop different approaches depending on the underlying function or purpose. If the purpose of the lying, say, is to obtain attention, we might regularly remind the child to ask for positive attention throughout the day. We'll address lying in detail in Chapter 4.

3. **Understanding the child behind the behavior problem is critical.** The behavior alone, isolated from the real child and his context, background, personality, and genes, does not make much sense. But if we pair the AFK youth's behavior with a discovered function, or functions, it will lead us in a direction where the puzzle pieces begin to fit together.

4. **To understand childhood behavior problems one must consider multiple causes.**[7]

5. AFK (Adoptive, Foster, or Kinship) parents are well positioned to positively influence the numerous challenges AFK children bring to their home. It is important for parents to understand that the relationship they establish with an AFK child is a powerful teaching and healing tool. Social learning theory recognizes that parents can create change and "capitalize on both the homelike foster family setting and proven methods of behavior change."[8]

A core theme in this book is that if we pair the AFK youth's behavior with a discovered function, it will help us understand the behavior, and then parents will be more successful in dealing with the behavior. Each chapter expands on this theme with specific reference to a complex, challenging behavior displayed by AFK youth.

Here is a sneak preview of each chapter.

Chapter 1, Introduction: "The Collision between the AFK Child and the AFK Parent" Meet two foster families and the two children they parent in foster care. Read about what motivated the families to become foster parents and how their motivations for doing foster care do not match-up with the hopes of the foster children they serve. Parents will also begin to understand the function and purpose of behavior as seen through the eyes of the child.

---

7 Bandura & Goldman, 1995; Cone, 1997; Haynes & O'Brien, 1990

8 (Chamberlain et al. 1990)

Chapter 2, "Hoarding Food, Hungry for Survival"
Patti has become an excellent food hoarder. She can take, hide, and, in isolation eat the fruits of her hoarding, which she finds comforting. In this chapter the connection between child neglect and hoarding will be established, and strategies suggested for parenting a child who hoards food.

Chapter 3, "Wetting Behavior; When It Rains It Pours" Why would any child sleep in a wet bed? What purpose could bedwetting serve? There are many reasons a child uses behavioral wetting. Children wet as an outlet for anger, to replicate the home environment, and for safety reasons. Parents will explore these, and other, reasons for bedwetting and learn how to positively manage behavioral wetting.

Chapter 4, "Lying and Stealing" Are you afraid your child will spend life in jail because of stealing? Are you angry because your child lies to you, even when the child doesn't need to lie? Often lying and stealing work together, frustrating the AFK parent to the point where trust is destroyed. This chapter will explain the connection of lying and stealing and the impact of both behaviors on the parent-child relationship.

Chapter 5, "Defiance May Not Be What it Appears to Be" Defiance is one of the major challenges that parents face while parenting AFK youth. Behavior that is "in your face" can provoke, challenge, and cause the parent to feel frustrated and over-reactive. Children can be defiant for different reasons, and this requires different interventions.

Learn how to determine which defiance you may be facing and how to understand and respond appropriately.

Chapter 6, "Naughty, Naughty, Relentless Negative Behavior" Children that negatively seek attention drain parents to the point that they question if they have anything else to give. These children are experts at creating parental exhaustion. Days are engulfed in responding to the child's overt and covert demands to respond to ME! Gain more information on how to redirect negative attention-seeking.

Chapter 7, "The Wisdom of the Experts" Stories from child welfare workers, adult former "systems" children and their parents will surprise and inspire you. One former foster youth describes how he would plan to disrupt placements if he felt unsafe. Another former foster youth explains the importance of ethnic identification. The story will be told of a young sexual abuse victim who, through a creative and caring foster mother, experiences a healing intervention for self-stimulation.

CHAPTER 1

Introduction: The Collision between the AFK Child and AFK Family

Wanting to Serve

Many of us value serving others. Helping children who have had unbelievably difficult beginnings in their short lives is especially of value to us. Many of these children end-up in foster care, kinship care, or adoptive homes because of their inability to live with their biological families. They bring with them many adaptations they have made to their difficult lives. These adaptations have functions that are exhibited as challenging behaviors. These behaviors are often difficult for the AFK (Adoptive, Foster, or Kinship) parent to understand. Often the AFK child's behavior is interpreted by the parents as a personal attack, when, in reality, it is not. A core issue in AFK parenting is that the background and journey of how the child and parent came to live together is often strikingly different.

Bob and Shirley Take-Up the Call to Serve

Bob and Shirley are a couple in their early 50's. They have reached a point in their life where their business is secure and their own children are grown and independent.

Shirley's first love is being a mother and a homemaker. She recognizes she is happiest when surrounded by her children and involved in their activities. Not that there haven't been difficult times. One of their sons was diagnosed with Attention Deficit Disorder while in elementary school. Shirley worked hard to support her son and understand ADD. Through a partnership with their son's school, and various helping professionals, their son eventually did well. Bob and Shirley learned a lot from this experience and the experience of parenting in general.

It is difficult for Shirley to understand why parents do not properly care for their children. She occasionally reads newspaper reports of families who abused or neglected their children. It is appalling to her. How could she help these unfortunate children?

Occasionally, Shirley would read foster parent recruiting ads and think about foster parenting. She discussed her interest with Bob, who was initially reluctant. Eventually, he became more open to the idea of foster parenting. Their minister's family was licensed as foster parents in the past, and encouraged Bob and Shirley to consider becoming licensed as foster parents. Shirley, with Bob's support, contacted their local County Social Services Agency and made an appointment to inquire about foster parenting. They agreed to pursue licensing and were amazed at the amount of work required. There was the licensing study accompanied by a number of interviews with the foster care social worker. Their initial foster parent training was interesting, and increased their desire to become licensed. Finally, they received their license and were placed on an active list for foster care placements. Bob and Shirley were excited about being able to open their home to a child in need.

Matt's Unstable Stability

Matt is a ten-year-old who lives in the same town as Bob and Shirley. Their paths have never crossed, as they reside in different parts of the community, both geographically and socially. Matt lives with his mother LuAnn, and her boyfriend, Pete. Matt's biological father has never been involved with Matt and his mother doesn't know where he lives. Matt has a younger half-sister named Theresa, but she lives with her father. Matt's Mom tries to have Matt and Theresa spend time together, which Matt enjoys. Matt has noticed that Theresa never comes to his home; he always goes to Theresa's home. Matt doesn't know why, but he thinks it may have something to do with Pete; Pete has a bad temper. More than once, Pete hit Matt when LuAnn and Pete were fighting. When Matt thinks that Pete is going to hit his mother, he always tries to get Pete's attention so he will hit him and not his mom.

Chapter One

Matt loves his mother deeply. She always tells him that someday things will be better. Matt loves it when his mother talks about how someday she'll have a good job, they'll have a house with lots of friends, and possibly Theresa living with them as a family. They both share this dream together. Unfortunately, Matt cannot be a "real" child around his mother. He can't express doubts about her optimistic view of the future, though he's starting to have some pessimism himself from time to time. He can't just say what he worries about. He can't confront his mother or express his concerns about the discrepancy between her pie-in-the-sky dreams and her day-to-day failings. That would hurt her. That might kill the dream.

Matt is a smart young man. He does OK in school, but where he really excels is in his understanding of adults and how to adjust to them. He is people smart. If Matt sees his mother and Pete staying up for days at a time he knows that he will have to take care of himself and also stay out of their way, especially Pete. Although Matt hates to admit it to himself, and never admits it to anyone else, he knows these are the times that his mother and Pete are using drugs. During these times Matt takes as much food as he can find and hides it in his bedroom. He also takes food from classmates and hides it at home. He's a survivor. Because, in the past, when his mom and Pete have been "using," there would be days when there wasn't any food in the home. Matt also knows when Pete's friends are at their home late into the night, it is better if he sleeps in a small fort that he makes in his closet. More than once someone has thrown Matt out of his bed so they could sleep in it. This was terrifying for Matt. It was, at these times, when Matt would become scared at night, that he began wetting his bed as he slept. Matt is very embarrassed by his wetting and tries to hide it to the best of his ability. Matt has learned a lot about living his life secretly. He knows that there are times when Pete brings home a lot of money. This is usually before Pete and LuAnn start "using." Matt found where Pete hides his money; when Pete and LuAnn are away from the home, Matt takes some of the money to buy things that he needs. He's always careful to not take too much. Matt has specialized in keeping a low profile. He lives his life beneath the radar screen, "low profile" you might say. His is a "secret and solitary" world.

Instability Wins

Recently, something odd happened at school. Matt's teacher said someone wanted to talk with him and they were waiting in a room by the principal's office. Matt had never seen this person before; she introduced herself as Bonnie. Bonnie was really nice to Matt but she asked a lot of nosey questions about Matt's home, his mother, and Pete. Some of Matt's answers were lies, because he would be in trouble if he told the truth. Matt knows how to spin the truth from years of living with volatile Pete. After Matt talked with Bonnie he ran home as fast as he could. He told his Mom about Bonnie and she wanted to know everything Matt said. Matt grew anxious about the third degree his mother gave him. He felt under pressure and cross-examined by her. So, he spun the truth a bit to try to reduce his mom's noticeable anxiety. He worried he'd get in trouble. Then Matt's Mom did something that seemed strange to Matt. She hurriedly cleaned the house, and they went out and bought groceries and spent a good part of the evening at the laundromat washing clothes.

Matt and his mother talked a lot about their dreams of having their own house, friends, Theresa, and being together as a family. This always made Matt feel happy. Within a couple of weeks things returned to how they were before Bonnie talked with Matt at school.

Matt could tell that Pete and his mother were getting ready to "use" again. Call it a sixth sense. Call it emotional radar, whatever. Matt anticipates problems. His antenna picks up the vibrations around him. (Interestingly, Matt is so focused on external matters and on picking up clues, he has little time or experience with understanding his own feelings.) Pete had money and a lot of Pete's friends were coming and going from the house. Matt was ready; he had food and money stored in his room and he knew he would need to start sleeping in his fort. As Matt was preparing his fort, he heard a burst of yelling and his mother start screaming. Before he could get into his fort two police officers entered his room. They took him to the police station, where he again saw Bonnie. Matt was scared for himself, but more importantly, for his mother. He was so scared he couldn't ask any questions, he only listened as Bonnie explained to him that he would be staying with another family, named Bob and Shirley. When Bonnie asked Matt if he had any questions, he was only able to ask one. "When can I go home to my mom?" Bonnie wondered if Matt missed his mother or worried about her. She'd seen so many children who were actually the caregivers of their own parent.

The Call to Service is Answered; Unwillingly by the Served

Bonnie had talked with Bob and Shirley, the newly licensed foster parents, earlier in the evening. She had asked them if they would be open to a possible emergency placement, and they agreed. In her follow up call, Bonnie indicated that she knew little about the child coming to their home, but to her knowledge he had no special needs. She told them that his name is Matt and that his mother had been arrested for possession of narcotics with intent to distribute. Bonnie indicated that she had interviewed Matt approximately one month ago on an allegation of child neglect. She also indicated that she had followed up with an in-home interview with his mother and could not substantiate child neglect.

Bob and Shirley were both excited and nervous about Matt coming to their home. Shirley re-checked the bedroom where Matt would be staying to make certain everything was neat and orderly. As she looked over the room, she thought to herself how sad it was that a mother would select drugs over her child.

As Bonnie waited at the police station for Matt's emergency placement order to be finalized, she received a call on her cell phone. The call was from one of her colleagues who was also on-call for the weekend. The call was not good news; her colleague informed her that he had to place one of the children in her foster care caseload, Angela, in shelter care, because of an aggressive episode at the foster home. Bonnie arranged for her colleague to finish the emergency placement of Matt with Bob and Shirley so that she could follow up with Angela's foster family.

Chapter One

Bonnie is formally introduced to Angela

Bonnie had known Angela for only six weeks. Angela had entered the foster care system through the juvenile justice system. Angela was arrested for shoplifting at a local grocery store. Even though she was only eleven years of age, Angela made a significant impression on the police as they intervened at the grocery store. She initially cooperated with the police, telling them that she hadn't taken anything, but rather, it was her friend and that the store security officer had falsely blamed her for the theft. When the police reviewed the video, it was apparent that it was Angela. In fact, they couldn't locate any "friend" with her. When presented with this information, Angela attempted to run from the police and used every physical and verbal means possible to escape. The police took Angela home after the incident, as her home residence had no phone. When they arrived at the apartment where Angela lived, no one was home. Angela insisted that she could stay there by herself but the police told her they could not allow her to do so and they would have to place her in temporary foster care until her mother contacted them. Unfortunately, Angela's mother never did contact them.

Angela Doesn't Like Formal Introductions

The results of Bonnie's search for information on Angela were sketchy at best. Through a regional child abuse information search she was able to find one alleged report of child abuse from approximately two years ago that named Angela as a possible victim. The anonymous report alleged that Angela was living in a home where there was suspected domestic violence. By the time child protective services initiated the investigative process the apartment was vacant and the landlord did not know where the family had gone.

Bonnie's effort to obtain information from Angela was unsuccessful. Angela only reported her mother as next of kin. Bonnie attempted to secure information from her school, but Angela was not enrolled in her neighborhood elementary school. She was able to contact Angela's previous elementary school but learned that she had only been at that school for two months and they provided little information. The school reported that in the two months Angela attended their school, there were two incidents where Angela had stolen from classmates and several incidents in which Angela had been assaultive to other children. Additionally, Angela had made several racially derogatory remarks to her Hispanic teacher. The school counselor indicated they had tried to set up several meetings with Angela's mother but she did not respond.

Angela Works for Herself;
AFK Parents Need Not Apply

Bonnie was struck by how Angela was always interested in what was going to happen to her, but it was not connected to any questions about her mother. Angela had been placed with an experienced foster family, Nate and Darlene. Angela did not want to stay with them because they were "mean." It seemed that "mean" meant having a minimum of rules in the home regarding attending school, doing chores, appropriate language, and engaging with the foster family.

Bonnie wanted to make an in-person contact with Nate and Darlene the evening that Angela had left their home for detention. She knew that they had worked hard to incorporate Angela into their family and that the placement had been difficult from it's beginning. When she arrived at their home, they were anxious to talk with her. It was obvious that they were upset, displaying a mixture of anger and hurt. They reported to Bonnie that Angela had come home from school late that day and had missed dinner as a result. When they asked her for an explanation, Angela responded by swearing at them and by telling them it was none of their business. They then escorted her to her room for a time-out. While in her room Angela ripped down the drapes, pulled out all of the drawers and dumped the contents on the floor. She also urinated on some new clothes that Darlene had recently purchased for her. When Nate and Darlene went to Angela's room to discontinue her time-out, she spit on Darlene and kicked Nate several times, prior to running from their home. She was apprehended by the police several blocks away.

Being Fired by Angela

As Nate and Darlene talked with Bonnie they described Angela as a child who had seemed to do well in their home for the first two weeks. They told Bonnie how Angela could be exceedingly charming when she wanted something, especially if it was an extra privilege or a material item. They were struck by how quickly this could change and how she could become argumentative and mean at a moments notice. They had been able to respond to these challenges at first but they could tell that Angela was quickly becoming less amenable to their parenting. As Angela became more distant and disruptive Nate and Darlene noted other behaviors that concerned them. They noticed that she would intentionally hurt their dog, to the point that they were scared to leave her alone when she had access to their family pet. Also, Nate was very concerned about a couple of incidents where Angela had said things to him that were sexualized. He said that these comments seemed tied to Angela wanting an exception to be made to a rule and were part of a bid to negotiate the rule. Nate indicated that he had immediately told her that her comments were inappropriate but it left him both uncomfortable and feeling at-risk for false reporting. Although Nate and Darlene were concerned for Angela, they both acknowledged that she had converted their home into a setting where they felt constantly on guard, tentative in their parenting, and worried about how Angela might respond to any given situation.

Why Collisions Take Place

The stories of Matt and Angela may sound all too familiar to experienced AFK parents and child welfare workers. The behavioral adaptations they both formed in childhood may seem bizarre, but when seen within the context of their environment they make sense and could even be viewed as sophisticated and purposeful. Unfortunately, they are not adaptations that create a healthy progression into adulthood. Examples of the adaptations displayed by Matt include food hoarding, stealing, secretiveness, provoking to protect, wetting, and lying. Angela's adaptations included stealing, lying, sexualized behavior, secretiveness, aggressiveness, distancing, manipulation, intimidation, and lack of attachment.

Many foster parents enter fostering for the same reasons as Bob and Shirley. They have a genuine desire to parent youth who are unable to be with their own families. Generally, this is a result of believing that they have something to offer AFK children based on their own parenting experience or their own growing up experience. Often these experiences are a mixture of positive experiences and possibly some difficulties that created growth, resulting in a commitment to the belief that the family is a positive, powerful force in the lives of children. Unfortunately, youth that enter AFK (Adoptive, Foster, or Kinship) care often have experienced the family as a negative force, rather than as a positive one.

Matt's history denotes a young man who has had to place intense attention on the issue of safety. In entering Bob and Shirley's home, it is realistic to think that Matt's need for safety would increase dramatically. Being separated from his mother and being worried about her status, being moved to a strange home, living with a family whose structure and routine is unfamiliar, and his continuous desire to go to his own home are strong reasons Matt may have for the need for increased safety. Considering Matt's "adaptations," it is realistic to expect him to replicate some of his safety behaviors. It would be reasonable to expect stealing, hoarding of food, and sleeping where he felt protected. These behaviors are probably not the type of behaviors that Bob and Shirley would expect in response to their providing a safe and stable home. The foster parents hadn't even considered that their home would be seen as unsafe by a foster child. Bob and Shirley approached foster care from the perspective that Matt would trust them, openly share his feelings with them, and appreciate that they were opening their home to him. However, Matt's perspective on adults, carried into the foster home, is that they might be a threat to him and his mother, that his communication with adults needs to be modeled around protecting himself and his mother, and that he carries primary responsibility for meeting his basic needs.

Although Nate and Darlene are more experienced than Bob and Shirley, their reasons for continuing to provide foster care probably remain rooted in believing that their values and their own family experience can benefit a foster child. Unfortunately, Angela enters their family with a grossly diminished ability to be cared for. Her world is viewed through the misuse of others to meet her own needs. Angela uses either coy interactions or aggression if she feels threatened or controlled. Children such as Angela are often viewed as delightful and yet dangerous. While Matt is an internalizing youth attempting to meet his needs through arranging and planning, Angela is an externalizing youth seeking need fulfillment through the control and domination of others.

There is no perfect family. However, Bob, Shirley, Nate and Darlene have worked hard to establish a family environment that nurtures positive relationships. In their family system, family members know that they are cared about and that dependability results in mutual trust, love and commitment. This is vastly different from the family experience of the AFK child's family system of unpredictability, fear, and, all too often, child exploitation. The diagram on page 32 further illustrates the dramatic differences between a healthy AFK family experience and the experience of many AFK children.

Collisions Are Needed and Necessary

AFK (Adoptive, Foster, or Kinship) parenting is a very complex and challenging role for even the most functional families, and the service they provide is generally under-recognized and under-appreciated. If at all possible, AFK children deserve the opportunity to be cared for in a community, with a family, and as an active participant in their care. However, in order to be effective as a parent, there must be an understanding that the parent's background and values will seldom be the same and accepted by the child that enters their home. Additionally, the AFK child feels this new home has been "inflicted upon him and against his will," rather than seen as an effort at providing a caring and stable home for a child in need. Both Matt and Angela need the care provided by the foster parents, but may not be able to benefit from it. It is important that parents understand this, so that they do not overly personalize the child's responses to their helping efforts. These collisions between caregiver and child are inevitable. Although it is almost impossible not to personalize a child's rejection of the parent's efforts, maintaining an emotional cushion will be necessary to continue parenting the AFK child.

HEALTHY FAMILY FUNCTIONING	POTENTIAL RESULTS	PRIOR AFK EXPERIENCE	POTENTIAL RESULTS
Child's basic needs are met with consistent parental responsiveness	Child and parent form a partnership based on trust	Child's basic needs met with inconsistency, possibly negligent, or abusive response	Child learns to suspect parental response – begins to self-parent
Discipline is structured, predictable, and based on a learning model	Child integrates parental respect and mutuality in relationships	Discipline is harsh, inconsistent, and reactive	Child internalizes anger and hurt – develops maladaptive responses to adult authority
Parental communication is nurturing, clarifying, limit setting	Child trusts family as a unit of security and eventual clarity	Unpredictable family communication, can be exploitive, confusing, nearly absent, and abusive.	Child models parental communication Learns not to trust "what is being said" Negotiation remains an unlearned skill
Childhood misbehavior is seen in the context of development and part of individual needs	Self esteem grows through love, structure, and nurturance. Cooperation is seen as important as compliance	Childhood misbehavior is a cause for over-reaction or neglect	Child continues to distrust parental responsiveness - reactions
Parent and child roles are clear, defined, and yet allow for life change adjustments. Relationships continue to evolve in relation to maturity and developmental transitions	Family relationships are seen as a partnership and dependable. Responses are based on the needs of the individual and the needs of the family	Child and parental roles are confused, boundaries are unclear. Often becoming a dynamic in physical and sexual abuse	Child experiences ambivalent and confusing feelings. Establishes a "split" in being too mature in adult manners and too immature in relationships

Moving On

In the following chapters, we will isolate specific behavioral/emotional challenges that AFK youth bring to their placements. We will identify functions of the emotional/ behavioral challenges and interventions that can be helpful to parents. However, for the interventions to be successful, the AFK parents must view the child as presenting a complex mixture of challenges that hold purpose and meaning for the child. Additionally, parents must accept that the caring they provide will not be accepted on their time schedule, but rather on the time schedule of the child. Understanding and accepting these dynamics will tremendously enhance all of our efforts at providing hope and change to the challenges.

CHAPTER 2

Hoarding Food: Hungry for Security

General Introduction/The Big Picture:

Headline:

"Three-year-old survives for three weeks on pasta, mustard, and catsup."

Many of us read with dismay about the preschooler who was left alone when the mother was incarcerated. Alone, without anyone aware of her existence, this child survived for nearly three weeks dining on a few uncooked foods and condiments, until she was finally discovered by her birth father. How could a mother not tell others about her child? How did the child survive that long, alone? How will this ultimately affect her in the long run?

More children suffer from neglect in the United States than from physical and sexual abuse combined. In spite of this, neglect has received significantly less attention than physical and sexual abuse and is often overlooked by practitioners, researchers, and the media. One explanation may be that neglect is so difficult to identify. Neglect often is an act of omission, the absence of an action. But neglecting a child's needs can be just as injurious as striking out at them.[9]

How does neglect impact hoarding?

The study of child development places a high degree of attention on the process of feeding in infancy. It is one of the primary interactions between parent and child, especially during the first year of life.[10] Not only is food a necessary source of life for the infant, but it is an important vehicle for emotional bonding and the development of language and social interaction. To put it in simple terms, when an infant cries for a bottle, and the parent responds with cuddling the infant and feeding them, they are fulfilling several basic needs. The parent provides food in response to hunger, develops attachment through nurturing, and develops trust through a predictable response. Ideally, food and feeding are recognized as important by the parent, and eating is pleasant on multiple levels for the child.

So what happens if the child is not well cared for? At a minimum, the child is forced to become pre-maturely self-reliant in meeting their own basic needs. For example, take

---

9 IN FOCUS: Acts of Omission; An Overview of Child Neglect, 04/2001

10 Child Development Institute, 04/25/2004

a parent who is severely chemically addicted and is inconsistent in providing meals and having food available. When food is available, a child sees this as an opportunity. It is logical that the child would respond to the availability of food in self-reliant ways, which could include over-eating and hoarding food in secretive ways.

All of us are creatures of habit. Our behavior, and the way we emotionally respond to situations, are patterns. We can change our behaviors and associated emotions, but it is difficult. This is especially true for behaviors that have worked for us. Hoarding food works for children that have been neglected. It feels good to have their hunger converted into fullness. It also feels good to know that they have food available in order to feed themselves in times of scarcity in the future. As a result, efforts of AFK (Adoptive, Foster, or Kinship) parents to change hoarding behavior are not easily accomplished. Progress is often inconsistent with a mixture of gains and set-backs. However, there are some interventions that have been received with success, especially with younger children.

Case in Point: Patti

Patti is a seven-year-old girl who has been in 18 different placements in her short life. These placements were a combination of relative placements, reunifications, foster care, shelter care, and finally treatment foster care. Although the caseworker didn't know much about Patti, one thing was certain. Patti had experienced a great deal of neglect, especially in her infancy.

Chapter Two

Shortly after being placed in treatment foster care, the foster parents began to notice that food was missing from their kitchen. When questioned, Patti denied having taken any food. In the same time period they began noticing the food missing, the school contacted the foster parents about Patti taking food from other students during lunch and also during snack time. At school, the teachers found that Patti's desk and locker contained hidden food. The foster parents checked Patti's room and behind a dresser, they found food stores covered by a rug. They also found food in her closet and drawers, all carefully concealed. They had noticed that at meals Patti often over-ate and seemed unable to feel when she was full.

That evening at dinner, the parents told Patti what they had found. Patti did not respond to their questions about why she had taken the food. They assured Patti she could have snacks and reasonable helpings at meals, but they wanted her to eat in the kitchen. Regularly, the foster mother checked Patti's room for food, and a week later, once again, they found hidden food. The mother contacted the school and her teacher reported that Patti was continuing to take food from other students.

CLINICAL INTRODUCTION/CLINICAL SNAPSHOT

Food hoarding and other peculiar food issues are rampant in AFK children. Food issues can be central in a child's world, and resistant to change. Parents don't understand why the issues continue when they have provided food for the child, consistently. Parents ask themselves, "Why does she gorge herself when we offer her seconds and even thirds for dinner?"

The short answer is neglect. The long answer is that the neglected child has had to become self-reliant in response to no, or little, parenting by the neglectful family.

Translated to the AFK (Adoptive, Foster, or Kinship) home, the child feels insecure, unworthy of care, and lacks trust with parents. They do not believe they will be cared for by the new family. If we think about a child "stealing" food, it doesn't acknowledge that there are other issues of neglect factoring into the behavior. The hoarding behavior is not merely an act of dishonesty, simple naughtiness, or an inability to understand right from wrong. The child doesn't believe his AFK parents will meet his needs, but instead thinks the parent is an obstacle to overcome, bypass, or outwit in meeting his needs.

FORM FOLLOWS FUNCTION
Figuring Out How Hoarding Works for the Child

Most problem behaviors serve a function. They work, or have worked in the past, to benefit the child in some way. Sometimes it's not so obvious to the casual observer. Even for experienced parents, it takes looking beyond the obvious to find the function.

Children may hoard food to:
- Reduce anxiety related to starvation
- Self-soothe as a result of poor nurturing
- Seek parental attention
- Meet their own needs, if the child is unable to ask or demand what is needed

AFK FAMILY INTERVENTIONS
Changing Scarcity into Abundance

It is important to remember the connection with neglect when designing interventions for hoarding behavior. Many of the AFK home interventions are designed to move food from an object of scarcity and secrecy to an object of abundance and openness. The goal is to build the trust in the parent-child relationship so that the child can allow the parent to meet his needs.

Let's get back to the case of Patti, who was hoarding food at home and school. This child continued to hoard, even when reassured by the parents that she would have plenty of mealtime food and also could have snacks. The initial intervention by the parent had missed some of the functions of the food stealing/hoarding. While reassurances may have reduced anxiety related to starvation, it did not address the issues of self-soothing, the secret-solitary habit, or possible negative attention-seeking. The parents may need to add some additional approaches with Patti to see how she responds.

Here are some approaches that might be tried:
- Food baskets
- Backpacks
- Flexible rules about food
- Coupling nurturing with food
- Bedtime rituals involving snacks

Let's take a closer look at these interventions.

Food baskets

Food baskets are often effective for kids who hoard food. The food basket consists of snacks that are healthy, but also appeal to the youth. Allow the child to choose the snacks for the basket, provided the choices are healthy. If the child is hoarding food in school, having a duplicate basket at the school is important.

It's important to explain why you are creating a food basket. Make it clear that food can be taken from the basket whenever the child is hungry. The child should be able to access the basket at any time, whether it is in the home setting or the school setting. Adults need to consistently fill the baskets and encourage their use. If you fear that the child will take the whole basket, you may want to implement some pre-established "Basket Rules." For example, the basket can be refilled daily so that the food is not unlimited. The child should be praised for taking food from the basket rather than hoarding food elsewhere.

Food baskets respond to the function of hoarding by:
- Reducing anxiety surrounding starvation through visual, consistent availability of food
- Creating openness in eating vs. eating as a secret-solitary activity
- Positively interrupting hoarding as a child's survival strategy

Backpacks

Kids today seem to use backpacks for everything. Backpacks carry books, CD's, school supplies, changes of clothes, make-up, and many other items. In many ways, the backpacks of today have replaced the lunch boxes and purses of yesterday. Having a food backpack can be a helpful way to help a child feel more secure and reduce hoarding. A separate backpack can be used, or a portion of a compartment in the child's backpack, for food storage. The backpack has the added bonus of being mobile and can be a socially acceptable modification for the child.

Like the food basket, some ground rules can be applied.
- Allow the child to choose some or all of the items
- Adults must consistently re-fill the backpack
- Teachers and other helping professionals shoud know about the backpack and be supportive of the strategy

Backpacks respond to the function of hoarding by:
- Providing the child with "traveling food security," which will reduce anxiety
- Allowing the child to remain self-reliant in a pro-social manner
- Positively interrupting the hoarding behavior as a primary survival strategy of the child

Flexible Rules on Food

Many of us grew up with identifiable rules and rituals regarding food. It is common to have family rules like no eating snacks between meals; finish everything on your plate; no eating before mealtime; and eat only in the kitchen. We also have pleasant memories of rituals that included food associated with birthday celebrations, special holiday foods, ice cream cones on a hot summer day, and special treats that only Grandma would make for us. There is nothing wrong with the food rules mentioned and the rituals are generally very pleasant memories.

But none of those rules or rituals was associated with deprivation and the neglect of food which threatened our survival as a child. It is always important to remember that hoarding food is directly related to neglect and hoarding food enabled the survival of the child. So before a child that hoards food will be able to respect an AFK (Adoptive, Foster, or Kinship) family's rules regarding food, they first must have repetitive proof that their basic need for food will be met. This doesn't mean that a foster family throws all their "food rules" out the window. But it does challenge a family to rethink their rules for a child who has been deprived of food. For example, if you don't want your child to ruin their appetite for dinner with extra snacking, you may want to provide a healthy snack at a reasonable time each day before dinner. You are reinforcing that food is available for the child, while still structuring an appropriate routine for dinner.

Flexible food rules:
- Reduce anxiety for the child
- Offer, via parents, a welcome attitude towards food
- Show that parents understand that food is an important issue for the child
- Model positive problem solving initiated by the parent
- Reduce the opportunity for food becoming the source of misbehavior
- Positively reduces hoarding as a survival strategy for the child

Coupling nurturing with food

Offer ample praise as the child begins to use a food basket or backpack in a healthy way. Tell the child how you like having the child in your home, recognize something special, or provide an appropriate expression of physical attention. This will provide the child with an opportunity to not only feel good because food is available, but also because an adult cares. For infants or younger children, you may want to feed them as they sit in your lap or as they sit closely to you. Having a child's hunger needs met should feel good for youth on multiple levels. Nurturing a child with food establishes eating as a positive, social, and life-giving activity.

Bedtime Rituals

Unfortunately, too many youth in foster care have not had a consistent caring adult in their life to nurture them, correct them, and assist with structuring their life's routine for them. With many AFK youth, a caregiver almost has to exaggerate those activities in an attempt to make up for the ramifications of neglect.

With pre-teen youth, spending time at bedtime with the child can be rewarding for all parties. Parents can talk about the special things that happened in the day, share a snack, and perhaps a bedtime story. Parents can also include "things that could go better" in the conversation, but this should be minimized to reduce distress. At these times, recognize improvement in hoarding and how you as a caregiver appreciate it. Reinforce how successful the child has been in changing his or her behavior.

Differential diagnosis

It's also important to consider that food issues may be related to underlying medical conditions. There are metabolic disorders and other conditions that can affect how, what, and how much the child eats. Your doctor will need to rule out such conditions as diabetes, hypoglycemia, Prader-Willi syndrome, etc. In addition, if your child takes a psychotropic medication, it may have the side effect of diminishing or increasing appetite, depending on the medication. Clinical depression can also impact eating. In clinical depression, appetite can be manifested in two ways; either through decreased or increased appetite.

There are a variety of childhood psychiatric conditions, and corresponding diagnoses, that focus on eating as a primary symptom.

Examples of other psychiatric conditions are:
- Pica (eating of non food substances)
- Rumination Disorder (where the child regurgitates and re-chews food after feeding)
- Feeding Disorder of Infancy or Early Childhood (where prior to the age of six, the child fails to adequately eat to the point where it can jeopardize the child's health)
- Anorexia Nervosa (where there is an intense fear of gaining weight which results in severely restrictive food intake)
- Bulimia Nervosa (marked by a pattern of binge eating, followed by self-induced vomiting)

In Adoptive, Foster, or Kinship (AFK) care, children commonly receive a diagnosis of Reactive Attachment Disorder. One of the major characteristics of Reactive Attachment Disorder is that a child views caregivers as objects unworthy of trust. Many children who have the diagnosis of Reactive Attachment Disorder have been chronically and severely neglected by their caregivers. As a result, numerous children with Reactive Attachment Disorder have learned to self-parent, and hoarding has been a successful means of survival for these children.

Parent Response to and Issues with Food

Sometimes our own issues surrounding food affect our ability to look at the child's problem with an open mind and creative flexibility. If a child in foster care returns from a visit to his biological family with the comment, "In my family we get to eat wherever and whenever we want in the house," it's likely to trigger some reaction in the foster parent. The foster parent may say, "Not in our house. We have rules about sitting at the table and eating with everyone else." Battle lines may be drawn where none were needed.

Instead, consider that the child may be saying:
1. I miss my own parents and the way we do things there.
2. I simply notice that there are differences between the households.
3. I'd like to fight with you about something.
4. I want to be noticed.
5. I find it hurtful and confusing to move from one home to another.
6. Whenever I see my parents, I worry about them afterwards and I feel grumpy.

If a foster parent responds casually, "Oh, that's interesting, but we still like to eat at the table at 5:00 when Dad gets home," chances are good that the control issue may disappear.

Remember that it is normal for children to regress in their behavior prior to and after visits with their biological parents. If the hoarding behavior has been reduced in your home, expect that it may reoccur following visits between the child and their biological family.

There are parental attitudes and responses that do not work for children who hoard food as a survival issue, which can include:

- If we as parents feel personally threatened, judgmental, and punitive about the child's eating issues, we are cooked.
- If we feel the need to exert control over how, what, when, where, and how much a child eats, we are cooked.
- If we feel personal failure "I'm not a good mother."
- If the parent's values feel disrespected by the child (e.g. child "steals" food), we are cooked.
- If we lock the pantry, the refrigerator, the kitchen, we create a "mine and yours" mentality, one the child is very familiar with from the past. We simply do not want to draw battle lines around food.

Rather than lockdown, perhaps look in the direction of feeding the child more often, and invite the child to have frequent snacks served up by us. This can take the battle out of this issue and re-educate the child about our partnership with them, and change food scarcity into abundance.

The combination of childhood neglect and trauma can create life time patterns. Most of us know individuals that have survived terribly tragic and life threatening circumstances. Most of these "survivors" go on to live productive, fulfilling lives. And yet, some of their trauma based adjustments stay with them forever.

As an example, consider the rancher who had lived through the devastating drought of the Depression. Having survived the Depression, no hay crop was ever sufficient enough for him. Even in good years, the fear of losing his cattle because of no feed continued to be an annual, pre-determined fear. In many ways, he became a hoarder of hay in order to assure the survival of himself, his cattle, and his family. This is similar for children that hoard food. Their almost nonsensical need for food security may lessen, even resolve, but it might also remain with them throughout their lives.

If you have issues surrounding food, examine how your child's eating problems might be triggering you. Ask yourself:
- Was I fed properly growing up?
- Did others feed me as my needs dictated?
- Did I compete with others for food?
- Was I given unhealthy messages about food or weight?
- Have I used food as a comfort or substitute for love?
- Does my own background influence the way I react to food issues?
- Is it interfering with an appropriate response to my child's hoarding?

In a comparison of healthy perspectives on feeding and food versus unhealthy food issues, the following perspectives could play out.

HEALTHY FAMILY PERSPECTIVE ON FOOD & FEEDING	POTENTIAL RESULTS	NEGLIGENT CAREGIVING IMPACT ON FOOD & FEEDING	POTENTIAL RESULTS
Infancy is marked by feeding needs met through consistent parental response, coupled with nurturing	Attachment is positively nurtured through life sustaining feeding	Food and feeding is neglected, inconsistent and absent in nurturing. Symbolic of general, substandard care.	Self-parenting issues around food begin early. Nurturance is absent from infancy feeding
Family models meal time as a sharing event	Feeding is consistent & meal time is a place of family joining	Meal time is unstructured, unpredictable or nonexistent. Double standard can be applied to "parent food" & "child food"	Food & feeding are solitary, "family absent" & self-focused
"Special" foods become celebratory-ex: birthday cakes	Food can become a part of pleasant, special family memories	Food is survival based, without celebration	Food becomes special in unhealthy ways- ex: hoarding, inability to regulate food intake
Food is available and a normal part of the family environment	Maladaptive responses to food are minimized	Food is scarce, or may be used as a vehicle of parental punishment	Feeding & food become solitary, self-protected, object of control

Final Remarks:

Hoarding may simply be a survival behavior, a vestige of early hardscrabble times in the child's life when it was hoard food or die. The key to designing parenting strategies lies in uncovering the function that the food hoarding has played in the past and continues to play in the present.

It's important always to look at an eating problem from various perspectives:
1. Could there be a biological or medical issue?
2. Does the child's history reveal reasons for fixation on eating?
3. Does the child substitute a food fixation for a loving relationship with parents?
4. What things trigger the child's eating problems?
5. Is the child displaying an emotional immaturity and neediness in the way he eats?
6. What are the conclusions the child has made about parent figures and how he views the world?

CHAPTER 3

Wetting Behavior: When It Rains, It Pours

General Introduction/The Big Picture:

At a recent foster/adoptive parent support group meeting, several parents were comparing war stories about children and their wetting problems. One father said that his foster son wet on his clean clothes in the dresser drawer. A foster mother topped that story with her foster daughter that had urinated in her purse. The prize winner, though, was the case of the child who, as the family slept, urinated in everyone's shoes.

One of the more difficult behaviors that AFK (Adoptive, Foster, or Kinship) youth bring to their placements is wetting behavior. These behaviors come in a variety of forms and can include bed wetting, wetting on self, urinating in containers such as jars and vases, urinating on clothes, in drawers or closets, urinating in corners of rooms, and urinating in vehicles. Some children even urinate down furnace vents. These behaviors are especially difficult for parents to manage and can often be a reason why a placement will disrupt. Child welfare workers and parents become frustrated because interventions for wetting behavior seem ineffective.

Case in Point: Carrie Protective/Anxiety Wetting

Carrie is a ten-year-old girl referred to treatment foster care by County Social Services. She was removed from her biological home because of sexual abuse. The abuse was perpetrated by a live-in boyfriend who is awaiting trial on the charges. The sexual abuse was confirmed medically. Carrie's mother is addicted to meth. Her whereabouts are currently unknown. The home was a known meth home, and occupied by a number of individuals who were using freely and often. Carrie has recently begun seeing a therapist in regard to her sexual trauma. She was in a County foster home. In the County foster home, it was noted that Carrie was urinating in jars at night and at times wetting her bed. There had been some day time wetting, but it is not consistent. She has been in a treatment foster care placement for approximately four months. The day time wetting has decreased as Carrie has adjusted to her treatment foster care home and new school. The night time wetting in containers and in her bed continues, but is decreasing in frequency. She remains a compliant, quiet girl who is hyper-vigilant; especially when encountering new people or situations.

CLINICAL INTRODUCTION/CLINICAL SNAPSHOT
Protective/Anxiety Wetting

In Carrie's situation, we know that she has been a victim of sexual abuse and subjected to extreme family chaos. Youth that have been sexually abused often become hyper-sensitive to sounds, smells, and risk factors in their environment. They also discover ingenious ways to protect themselves from very harmful, abusive adults. Night time is a high risk time for youth to be sexually abused. If we remember that from Carrie's perspective being placed into a new foster home means that she is living with strangers, it would also make sense that her first response to being alone, in a new home at night, would be to feel anxious and feel the need to protect herself. A child with a sexual abuse background such as Carrie would be taking a risk to leave her room and walk to the bathroom in the dark. The flush of the toilet would announce to all the other family members that she is alone and vulnerable in the bathroom.

For Carrie, it is much "smarter" to urinate in a jar. Additionally, Carrie can protect herself by wetting her bed and making herself unappealing to potential perpetrators who may be nearby.

Chapter Three

FORM FOLLOWS FUNCTION
Figuring Out How Protective/Anxiety Wetting Works For The Child

Protection/anxiety wetting works for the child because:
- By wetting on the bed and herself, she becomes unappealing to a potential threat.
- The child can remain safe and protected in a designated area.
- Protection/anxiety wetting can become a successful function that becomes a pattern and habit.

AFK FAMILY INTERVENTIONS
for Protective/Anxiety Wetting
Exaggerating and Proving Safety

In situations such as Carrie's, it is critically important to make the night time routine as safe and predictable as possible.
- Find out if the child is afraid to leave her bed at night and if those fears contribute to the wetting.
- Have the child help select night time lighting for her room and allow the child to arrange the bedroom in a way that helps her feel comfortable.
- Tell the child positive and comforting bedtime stories.
- Explain and show the child that the bathroom light will be left on and show the child the bathroom with the lights on.
- Provide the child with a flashlight. Review the pathway to the bathroom.

- Try to identify with the child symbols that help the child feel safe and strong. Examples of strong symbols could be special stuffed animals or night time prayers.
- Show the child that all windows in the bedroom are locked.
- Exaggerate and reinforce all safety measures, possibly every evening at bedtime, until the child shows increased confidence and feels safe.
- Have the AFK child use the bathroom prior to bedtime.
- Reinforce dry nights positively and respectfully.

Exaggerating and proving safety responds to the functions of protective/anxiety wetting:
- By allowing the child to experience safety on a repetitive basis so that wetting is no longer necessary.
- By positioning the AFK (Adoptive, Foster, or Kinship) parent as a dispenser of strength and safety rather than as a threat.
- By actively involving the AFK child in determining their own safety.

Don't re-traumatize wetting incidents

If a child comes to your home with protection/ anxiety wetting, chances are the wetting will not extinguish in the short-term. As a result, the way that the parents handle the wetting is important in their efforts to change the wetting behavior. If the parent uses a "waking" strategy to combat the wetting behavior, be certain that the child is woken in a safe and supportive manner.

Bedwetting alarms are a popular choice to combat wetting. But behavioral wetting is functionally different, and these devices may startle and alarm the child and not be effective. However, advances are being made in supportive mechanisms and devices that are more child-friendly and non-traumatic. Consulting with a pediatrician that has an interest in wetting behavior can assist with a review of these new developments.

Some other ideas for long term wetting:
- Use protective devices such as plastic mattress covers and disposable pads beneath sheets.
- Have extra pajamas available in the bedroom at all times. Store extra sheet sets beneath the mattress for quick changes.
- If wetting interventions fail, consider using a container like a camping porta-potty in the child's room.
- Reinforce dry nights positively and respectfully.

Not re-traumatizing wetting incidents responds to the functions of protective/anxiety wetting by:
- Demonstrating to the child that adults can be accepting and understanding of the child's challenges, without abuse.
- Modeling for the child that change is a process and not immediate.

Case in Point: Jenna Anger/Control Wetting

Jenna is a thirteen-year-old female currently living with her uncle and aunt in kinship care. Both of Jenna's parents are in prison for distribution of controlled substances. Jenna was physically abused and neglected by her parents. She has been cared for by a variety of relatives; they found Jenna very difficult to parent. Jenna returned to her parents several times, but never for a sustained period of time. Jenna is a child who is always on guard and is easily irritated. She is being treated with two medications, one that treats symptoms of mood instability, and a medication for attentional difficulties. Jenna does poorly in school, resists directives, fights with peers, and argues with teachers. She does best in the resource room where expectations are clear but not based on group conformity. Jenna enjoys physical activity and is active. In the school's resource room, she has developed the ability to impose a self time-out. Often, the time outs involve drawing or physical activities, completed alone. Generally, she can re-involve herself with others after these time-outs. Jenna sees an individual therapist but the therapist acknowledges that Jenna has been resistant to establishing a therapeutic relationship.

Jenna does not experience daytime or evening wetting. However, on several occasions, Jenna has taken her clothes, placed them in a pile and urinated on them. This usually happens when things are going well in the relationship with her uncle and aunt. Something seemingly insignificant happens and Jenna becomes angry, especially with her aunt. Jenna seems to enjoy being "caught" for urinating on her clothes, and seems to take pleasure in her aunt and uncle's angry and hurt feelings.

CLINICAL INTRODUCTION/CLINICAL SNAPSHOT
Anger/Control Wetting

Jenna is a youth who displaces her feelings of anger towards others. She can react with angry intolerance towards others. In Jenna's mind, it is better to reject others before they reject her. This may relate to her own feelings of abandonment and rejection. Often AFK parents are the primary targets of this relationship-intolerance. It seems that just when the child begins to feel their own defenses soften toward the AFK parent, they quickly retreat towards a position of extreme anger and rejection. This allows Jenna to maintain a safe distance from the AFK parents that care about her. In anger/control wetting, wetting is one of many dramatic means to keep a parent at arm's length.

FORM FOLLOWS FUNCTION
Figuring Out How Anger/Control Wetting Works for the Child:

- Anger/control wetting allows the child to maintain a safe distance from the AFK parents.
- It is a way to expend internalized angry feelings.
- Anger/control wetting can create parental confusion, hurt, and anger that distracts from consistency in parenting.

AFK FAMILY INTERVENTIONS
for Anger/Control Wetting
Focus Therapeutic Attention with the AFK Parents

In Jenna's situation, the parents should seek a professional who is well-versed in the dynamics of AFK children and attachment dynamics in children. As a team, the parents and the therapist can identify cues and triggers that indicate when Jenna is becoming uncomfortable with the closeness of the home. It's important to realize that Jenna often expresses anger from a displacing, indirect perspective. Through her wetting behavior, she doesn't get mad, she gets damp. Ideally, as the parents become skilled at "stepping back" when Jenna becomes uncomfortable, she will eventually learn alternative coping skills rather than through acting out by urinating on her clothes.

Focusing therapeutic attention with the parents responds to the function of anger/control wetting:

- By assisting the parents in understanding how to provide a safe distance for the child, which can diminish the expressions of angry rejection by the child.
- By providing the parents with support so they do not react to the child as have other adults, or through reciprocal rejection.

Identify Mechanisms That Have Been Successful in Helping the AFK Child Expend Energy

Jenna's school history suggests she enjoys solitary activities and physical activities. Physical activity enables Jenna to expend angry energy when she feels stressed and irritable. She has been able to self-regulate in school and self-impose time outs when needed. Jenna calms herself by utilizing physical activity and by drawing. She seems to have learned, through school-based interventions, how to reduce her anxiety level in terms of approaching adults who want to relate closely to her. As a result, it could be productive to build into Jenna's daily routine activities at home that expend energy. Rewarding her involvement in these activities and seeking other forms of expression that do not involve direct confrontation may be helpful for Jenna.

Identifying mechanisms that have been successful in helping the AFK child expend angry energy responds to the function of anger/control wetting:
- By being proactive in supporting the child in expending angry energy before it becomes problematic.
- By providing a consistent network of caring adults that respond in a similar manner to the child's struggle with anger within relationships.

Apply Consequences for Anger/Control Wetting
Teaching responsibility to an AFK child is a consistent challenge for parents. Consequences for misbehavior are a way to teach responsibility. But consequences lose their teaching component if they are applied in a harsh or punitive way. In these situations, the child will quickly dismiss the consequence as a product of "just another adult that will hurt them." In Jenna's situation, if the wetting is intentional and directed at hurting the parents, the parents may choose to consequence the wetting behavior but should proceed with caution. Consequence the intentional anger/control wetting

in a nonchalant, non-punitive, and non-shaming manner. Jenna could possibly clean and wash the clothes and the area where she urinated. The primary focus should remain on helping Jenna learn other mechanisms to express her anger.

Applying consequences for anger/control wetting responds to the function of anger/control wetting:
- By modeling for the AFK child that consequences for misbehavior can be delivered in a non-punitive, yet consistent manner.

Case in Point: Joey
Wetting That Is Reminiscent of Home

Joey is a fourteen-year-old young man who has recently been removed from his parent's home and placed in foster care due to physical, medical, and educational neglect. This is Joey's first placement away from his home. Both of Joey's parents are dually diagnosed, suffering from a combination of developmental disabilities and psychiatric disorders. Additionally, they are in poor health. Joey's birth family has received a variety of services, economic assistance, home health services, homemaker services, parent aide services, and CMI (Children's Mental Illness) and DD (Developmentally Delayed) case management services. Inspite of all of these services, and the best intentions of Joey's parents, the home remains unsanitary and neglectful. Joey is underweight and the home health nurse has identified that Joey is not receiving proper nutrition in the home. Additionally, Joey has been refusing to go to school and has not been attending. He says that the other students make fun of him because he smells and they call him dumb. Joey has been assessed with an intellectual deficit.

Joey loves his parents deeply. He wants to return home and talks about it constantly with his foster parents, his birth parents, his counselor, special ed. teacher, and social worker. He has regular visits with his parents, generally accompanied by his social worker. After the visits he cries and isolates himself in his bedroom at his foster home. Although he refuses to admit it, he has been wetting his bed in the evening. He also experiences daytime wetting which he does not acknowledge. The wetting escalates after home visits.

CLINICAL INTRODUCTION/CLINICAL SNAPSHOT
Wetting That Is Reminiscent of Home

Joey displays a significant attachment to his family. The attachment is compromised by the parent's inability to care for him because of their own limitations. Additionally, Joey doesn't completely understand why he can't be with his parents due to his and his parents' intellectual disabilities. For Joey, it is very simple; he just wants to go home.

It is very possible that Joey did not consistently have clean clothing and bedding available in his own home. In fact, sanitary smells may be foreign and possibly uncomfortable for Joey, especially if the new smells amplify his feeling of isolation from his parents. As humans, smells and physical feelings trigger memories for us, both pleasant and unpleasant. One possible function of Joey's wetting could be to recreate the atmosphere and memories of his home where he desperately longs to return.

FORM FOLLOWS FUNCTION
Figuring Out How Wetting That Is Reminiscent of Home Works for the AFK Child:
- Wetting allows the AFK child to recreate a sensory experience from their biological home.
- Wetting allows the AFK child to remain loyal to their biological family.
- Wetting can be a form of expression of sadness and anxiety over not being able to be with their biological families.

AFK FAMILY INTERVENTIONS
for the Reminiscent Wetting Model That Joey's Commitment to his Biological Family is Honored:

Because of Joey's limitations, he may not be able to understand that his biological family cannot care for him even though they love him. It is important that he feel from the AFK family non-judgment of his biological family and acceptance that they are his primary attachment. To model these attitudes to youth like Joey, attempt to establish a number of symbols and objects that can be transferred from Joey's bio-home to his bedroom in his foster home. Assure him that these items will stay with him, even as he leaves foster care. Objects and symbols can be pictures and videos of family, toys, personal security items, blankets, music, etc. AFK parents can support the child by being positively involved in the visitation with the biological family. For example, Joey and his foster parents cound deliver a pie they prepared together as a gift to his birth parents. This demonstrates to Joey and his bio-parents that the AFK parents are honoring his birth family.

AFK parents can show by example to Joey that he has a number of people who care for him in both his birth and AFK family. This can reduce Joey's feelings of split loyalty between his birth family and the AFK parents.

Modeling That Joey's Commitment to His Family is Honored Responds to the Function of Reminiscent Wetting:

- By showing the child that people involved in their AFK experience respect and honor the youth's birth family.
- May decrease stress that presents itself through wetting.
- Allows the child to replicate memories of their birth home in the AFK home, rather than replicate memories through wetting behaviors.

Talk and Teach Skills Associated with Wetting

In a situation like Joey's, the wetting behavior is probably partially tied to inconsistent attention on toileting skills. As a result, parents should work with Joey on toileting instruction and the teaching of proper hygiene skills.

This process should be visual, concrete, and repetitive. Exaggerate positive reinforcement for compliance and reward with concrete rewards that appeal to the AFK child. Openly blaming the child's biological family for the wetting behavior will probably cause wetting regression by the child.

Talking and Teaching Skills Associated with Wetting Responds to the Function of Reminiscent Wetting:

- By normalizing the wetting behavior as an unlearned skill so that responding to the wetting behavior can be

- instructional rather than consequence-based.
  - By isolating the wetting behavior as a skill to be learned rather than associating it with negative judgments on the youth's birth family.

Case in Point: Darwin
Wetting as a Symptom of Neglect

Darwin is a five-year-old child recently entering foster care because of parental abandonment. Little is known about his background as his birth family was new to the area prior to the child protection intervention. He experiences a number of developmental delays that often indicate child neglect. Darwin is scheduled for a variety of evaluatory appointments in the next month.

Darwin is a very active child; he never seems to stop. He runs everywhere, yells instead of talks, takes instead of asks, overeats to the point that he becomes ill, and has tantrums when matters do not go the way he wants. However, Darwin can be very loving and engaging given the right circumstances. It doesn't seem that he has been toilet trained. He doesn't seem to experience any discomfort in wetting his pants, or sheets, or anywhere else for that matter. His foster father attempted to have Darwin urinate in the toilet. Darwin urinated everywhere but in the toilet, and seemed bewildered by the toilet experience.

CLINICAL INTRODUCTION/CLINICAL SNAPSHOT
Wetting as a Symptom of Neglect

Like many youth when they first enter foster care, little is known about Darwin's background. We do know his behavior seems delayed, or behind, compared to most five year olds. It also appears that Darwin has been subjected to child neglect, as parental abandonment marked his entry into foster care. As we discussed previously, neglected children will learn to care for themselves or self-parent. When toileting is neglected, children become comfortable with being wet and do not develop the same intolerance for being wet as children that are properly toilet trained.

FORM FOLLOWS FUNCTION
Figuring Out How Wetting, as a Symptom of Neglect, Works for the AFK Child.
- The child does not depend on adults to help them with wetting because of repeated caregiver negligence.
- The child continues to self-parent because it works and has become a pattern.

AFK FAMILY INTERVENTIONS
Wetting When it is a Symptom of Neglect:

Recognize Toileting as a New Skill
In situations like Darwin's it is important to view toileting as a new experience for the AFK child. As a result, the child will need significant assistance and in-home programming. Begin the process by using the proper clothing and toilet fixtures. Consider using nighttime pull-ups and a potty chair. If using pull-ups, start the reinforcement process by rewarding Darwin when he acknowledges he is wet. After he is able to identify when he is wet, begin to schedule toilet-

ing for Darwin at certain time internals. If possible, review the schedule with a pediatrician. Ask for medical recommendations regarding fluid intake and ask about medication that can help to prevent wetting.

Structure and teach the child toilet skills:
- Throw cheerios in the toilet and have Darwin "shoot" at them.
- Include the school and day care center in the behavior programming to accomplish consistency.
- Verbally reward any success, especially when Darwin self initiates any toileting.

Recognizing Toileting as a New Skill Responds to the Function of Wetting as a Symptom of Neglect:
- By assisting the AFK child in learning skills not previously learned.
- By providing the AFK child and AFK families with a structured, progressive manner to respond to wetting behavior as a symptom of neglect.
- By showing the AFK child that they can rely on parents to teach skills without the process being reactive, punitive, or inconsistent.

Assessment Factors:
AFK youth that are displaying consistent wetting behavior, past an appropriate development age, should be evaluated by a qualified physician, preferably a pediatric urologist. Be selective when choosing the physician who evaluates the youth because of the potential connection of past childhood trauma and wetting. It is also important to

consult a pediatrician or child psychiatrist for a review of medication intervention options for wetting behavior or contributing medical conditions.

If an AFK youth is experiencing wetting behavior, try to obtain more information about the following:
- The nature of the wetting: patterns, settings where the child wets, what escalates/diminishes the wetting.
- Has the child been medically and psychiatrically evaluated for the wetting behavior, and what were the results?
- Was the youth ever toilet trained?
- Has the child experienced childhood trauma; e.g., sexual abuse?
- Was the child neglected and what was the nature of the neglect?
- Does the child have the intellectual ability to learn toileting?
- Is there a behavioral and/or emotional connection to the wetting that can be identified?
- Has there been any psychological testing or therapy that comments on the wetting behavior from a causation or intervention perspective?
- What interventions have been tried, and what were the results?
- What is the child's caregiver's response to wetting?
- Is there a history of wetting in the youth's family? If so, at what age did the wetting behavior stop?

Hopefully the history collected will assure that the AFK youth has received the proper medical and psychological evaluation for the wetting behavior. Also, securing and reviewing this information should help you establish insight into future interventions and avoidance of repeating past failed interventions.

Differential Diagnosis:

If there isn't a medical condition that is the primary cause of wetting, chances are good that the wetting is influenced by emotional factors. There are a variety of mental health conditions that could be associated with wetting behavior. For example, in considering the four functions of wetting behavior that are identified in this chapter, the following mental health conditions and diagnoses could be present in the chapter's case scenarios

Carrie: protective/anxiety wetting
- Depressive Disorders
- Anxiety Disorders
- Post Traumatic Stress Disorder
- Reactive Attachment Disorder

Jenna: anger/control wetting
- Oppositional Defiant Disorder
- Attention Deficit Disorder
- Disruptive Behavior Disorder
- Reactive Attachment Disorder
- Depressive Disorders
- Mood Disorder
- Post Traumatic Stress Disorder

Joey: reminiscent of home wetting
- Depressive Disorders
- Anxiety Disorders
- Adjustment Disorders

Darwin: symptoms of neglect
- Reactive Attachment Disorder
- Oppositional Defiant Disorder
- Attention Deficit Disorder

Parental Response to Wetting:

Wetting behavior can be aggravating, mystifying, and discouraging to parents that deal with wetting on a daily basis. It is very important for parents, therapists, and child welfare workers to look at the wetting from the perspective of what purpose and function wetting serves. Thoroughly understanding the child's background can offer answers to the function of the wetting behavior. Often the wetting behavior provides a function for the child in a neglectful or otherwise harmful environment. When the function of the wetting is understood, adults can design positive interventions that can work to replace the wetting behavior. Functional behaviors such as wetting are difficult to change because they work for the child. They can, however, be replaced through positive intervention strategies, consistency in routine, and tolerance for periodic regression.

As with so many challenges that youth bring to AFK care, the home and the child's experiences are mismatched. If we compare a healthy parental response to teaching toileting skills to a negligent or abusive response to teaching toileting skills, we might find the following:

HEALTHY FAMILY FUNCTIONING	POTENTIAL RESULTS	PRIOR AFK EXPERIENCE	POTENTIAL RESULTS
Parent's view toileting as a normal, developmental task	A proper context for toileting is set by the parents	A context for toileting is not defined or doesn't exist	Child's context is void. Soiling & wetting may adopt functions such as protection
Successful toileting is recognized & positively reinforced	Parents are attuned to the child's needs in learning a new task	Parental response can be negligent or inconsistent	Child's toileting models the parental response-inconsistent
Toileting "accidents" are seen as a normal part of learning	Flexibility in parental response is displayed	Parental response to "accidents" can be harsh or a non-response	Child becomes anxious regarding toileting. Avoids parental involvement
Mastery of toileting becomes a source of pride for the child	Child internalizes a sense of competence through a positive partnership with the parent	Consistent parental recognition of developing toileting skills is absent	Child lacks a partnership with the parent in learning. Mastery is evasive, not valued by the child
The purpose of toileting is defined as good hygiene & socially important.	Parents recognize the importance of a child's learning connected to purpose	The purpose of toileting is not taught & supported. Can become an expectation without reason	Secondary problems develop: negative recognition for poor hygiene
Successful toileting becomes a healthy routine for the child	Child is able to generalize success to other learning tasks	No healthy routine is established or recognized	Child's norm can become being comfortable with wetting & soiling

Final Remarks:

Wetting behavior is one of the more challenging behaviors that the AFK child may bring to the placement. Wetting can cause a home to smell, ruin beds, sheets, and carpets, and can control the life routine of a family. All of these factors attack the AFK parent's resiliency which can easily result in frustration, especially when considering how easily it seems the behavior could be changed. The good news is that wetting behavior usually stops or lessens unless there are medical or intellectual issues that prevent improvement.

It is our hope that this chapter has provided the AFK parents with information on assessment, functions and interventions for wetting.

CHAPTER 4

Lying and Stealing

General Introduction/The Big Picture:

Most adults believe the adage: "Honesty is the best policy." But, surveys with adults reveal that most lean towards telling "little white lies" when needed. For many average individuals, truth-telling is an ideal to shoot for, but truth is downsized, spun, or altered. In practice, most people are moderately honest and truth is provided on a "need to know" basis.

With AFK (Adoptive, Foster, or Kinship) children who are troubled, candor and fact are the exception more than the rule. Lying is a well-honed skill in some children, one that served them well in dangerous situations. Lying was a survival skill which served an essential function: keeping the child relatively safe.

Similar to lying, stealing often served the foster or adopted child well in the past. It may have provided basic necessities or it may have been an attempt to address the essential unfairness of a world filled with those who "have," and those who "have not." Often, lying and stealing go hand-in-hand. They can be twin problems—"Did you take my hat?" "No, I didn't." "What's that on your head?" In this chapter we cover both lying and stealing—the twins.

Some AFK children gravitate to compulsive lying and/or stealing. This is due to the emotional problems that stem from their prior abusive and neglectful backgrounds. Many foster parents wonder why these children continue to lie and steal, even though they are in the safe confines of a good family. Bowlby, in his earliest writings on the subject of attachment, pointed to the finding that children with presenting problems of "thievery" had suffered chronic separation and loss, and had come from extremely "disrupted" childhoods.[11] Thievery or other types of dishonesty do not simply evaporate after the child is placed in protective custody or living within a good AFK (Adoptive, Foster, or Kinship) home.

Typically, stealing and lying develop together. Deception covers thievery. Trickery conceals robbery. These twin problem behaviors, stealing and lying, effectively dissuade AFK parents from trusting their troubled child. As with other conduct problems, lying and stealing stem fundamentally from a negative working model, i.e. a view of caregivers as unreliable, unresponsive, and too threatening to negotiate needs.

---

11 Bowlby, John, The making and breaking of affectual bonds. New York: Tavistock Publications Limited, (1979)

Though they often are interrelated, let's separate out lying from stealing for the moment in the discussion of the following cases.

Stealing

While typical children and adolescents may steal during periods of temporary family crisis or as teenagers experiencing a temporary lapse in judgment or ethics, the AFK child steals habitually. Viewing the world as stingy, ungiving and unfair, this child feels justified in taking objects to balance out inequities, and even as a substitute for sparse or non-existent affection. Those who work with troubled AFK children soon find out how common stealing is. Indeed, countless individuals have been "ripped off" by these youth.

Case in Point: Barbie Stealing

Barbie, a recently placed foster child, seemed to be a model student in her fourth grade classroom. It must have been a coincidence that objects turned up missing throughout the classroom. After three months, however, the teacher discovered where all the missing objects had gone. The bottom of Barbie's desk was layered with extra pencils, notebooks, rulers, and glue which she had squirreled away. But no one had ever caught Barbie in the act of stealing.

CLINICAL INTRODUCTION/CLINICAL SNAPSHOT

For the AFK child, theft often stems from an underlying, pervasive feeling of deprivation and neglect. It also may relate to a level of on-going anxiety and insecurity. Some children truly do not feel calm and secure enough to ask for what they want, to assume that what they need will be supplied, and what they say will be listened to and addressed by caregivers. This child may experience deep resentment and bitterness over the fact that her needs have been chronically unmet.

In her mind, caregivers cannot be trusted to provide for her physically and emotionally, and so she must take matters into her own hands. Her sense of being neglected is pervasive. For Barbie, stealing objects at home or in school may be a way of expressing hostility towards individuals she perceives as being responsible for gross insensitivity and callousness. Upon examination, it was discovered that Barbie was insanely jealous over attention given by the teacher to other children; attention she felt was rightfully hers.

The troubled child may repeatedly loot the parent's bedroom, pilfering jewelry, pocket change, or intimate apparel. It is common for AFK children to steal wedding rings. On one hand, a troubled AFK child, desperate for attention, may harbor resentments over the foster parents' private relationship. Each time their bedroom door closes behind them, the child's anger is rekindled. On the other hand, the child, having been raised by a terrifying parent in the past, may eschew asking the foster or adoptive parents for things she either wants or needs. Instead, she secretly and silently takes.

Compulsive stealing, which often begins in the family of origin, can generalize to other settings outside the home, such as school, foster care, and the community at large. The child's perception of the world as scary, stingy, exploitive, and unreliable justifies the persistent stealing. The theft habit gradually grows more sophisticated and secretive and gives the child a perverse sense of mastery over others. "Putting one over" on others without getting caught offers the child some temporary satisfaction. What may originally have spurred the child to steal (for example, neglect), may morph over time to a new motive, (for example, fooling others). Unfortunately, as the child grows more adept at stealing, the underlying needs for affection, concern, and appropriate emotional response from loving adults remain unmet. Parent figures inevitably become more distant and more punitive because of the stealing. Stealing exacerbates the problem because it makes it even less likely that the child will ever receive what he needs, a therapeutic bond to a caring, giving adult. The child's first unfulfilling caregiver relationship is reenacted in the foster home.

With food stealing, as well as with theft of non-nutritional items, the child may have no current objective need for whatever is taken. From a survival point of the view, the behavior problem is obsolete. For example, when a child conducts midnight raids of the pantry and stockpiles the goods in his bedroom, this may be a reaction from when food was decidedly hard to come by. It's understandable when a formerly neglected and starved child takes food. What is more puzzling is a child's "pack-rat behavior," taking ostensibly insignificant items sometimes randomly without apparent use to him. This type of stealing seems to suggest a compulsive behavior, or that the child enjoys outwitting, and distancing herself, from the stingy adult world.

FORM FOLLOWS FUNCTION
Figuring Out How Stealing Works for the Child

After pinpointing the structure or form of the problem, we collect information on function. Ask the following question: why? When we seek to find out why stealing occurs, we need to return to our functions list. This will help us uncover the purpose, the point, the motive, the cause, and/or the function of stealing for the child.

The nine common functional behaviors related to stealing:

1. **ATTENTION:** A child gains and maintains attention, sometimes "negative attention," from interactions with others. *Example: A child steals something and others spend time cross examining him about the missing item(s).*

2. **ASKING FOR A NEED/WANT TO BE MET:** A child may be communicating a need or want, though sometimes in a roundabout way. *Example: A child fears asking for what he wants or needs, so resorts to stealing.*

3. **FEAR OR PHOBIA:** A child may have an automatic and powerful response to certain triggers or situations. *Example: A child is afraid of being abused so does not assert what he needs or wants.*

4. **AVOIDING OR ESCAPING:** A child's behavior may serve to help avoid or escape some undesirable event, task or individual. *Example: A child steals some desired object to get out of having to earn money to buy it.*

5. **REDUCE ANXIETY/PAIN:** May reduce tension or discomfort that a youth feels. *Example: A child feels a growing sense of pain about not ever having enough or about not being worthy of receiving good things, so he takes material goods to relieve the misery, at least temporarily.*

6. **PROVIDE STIMULATION/PLEASURE:** Behaviors are fundamentally rewarding and pleasurable. *Example: A child derives some satisfaction from outsmarting adults. He's good at it; he's a real pro. The child conceals valuables, and has expert ways of sniffing out hiding spots.*

7. **FAMILY ISSUES:** Issues in the family may result in certain behavioral problems in the youth. *Example 1: A child has watched his birth parents steal and he imitates the behavior. Example 2: Rampant neglect has left him feeling chronically deprived. He sees what other more fortunate children have. He is bombarded by TV ads about the latest, must-have toys and videogames, and he wells up with envy. Stealing follows. Stealing can be a self-parenting behavior. The child takes care of his/her needs in the absence of, or expected, negligence by a caregiver. Stealing can express anger in a relatively safe way, if you don't get caught. It can also be a surreptitious, retaliatory pay back to others.*

8. **PHYSICAL/MEDICAL:** Physical ailments and psychiatric or neurological disorders can produce certain problem behaviors or symptoms. *Example: A child with A.D.H.D. takes things impulsively with no thought for consequences.*

9. **COGNITIVE DISTORTION:** Some behaviors naturally spring from distortions in a youth's thinking or from irrational thoughts. *Example: A child's early experiences have caused him to conclude that it's better to take than to wait for someone to give.* (IBID, page 12)

It's important to recall that stealing can serve one or several purposes, and the purpose of purposes of stealing can evolve over time.

AFK FAMILY INTERVENTIONS

Here are some brief thoughts about interventions related to stealing. It's important to try to replace stealing behavior with functionally equivalent behaviors or with acceptable constructive options. In other words, our interventions and strategies should relate to the function.

Here are some examples:
Child's viewpoint and strategy

- **Expressing anger or vengefulness:** Give the child better forms of verbal expression. It's important to look at how adept the child is at speaking his feelings and thoughts assertively and directly to others.
- **The world is unfair:** Work to help the child express, insist upon, and negotiate for his wants and needs.
- **Self-parenting:** Anticipate the child's needs and wants and convince the child that we can help provide for needs.
- **Create excitement or attention getting:** Proactively provide interpersonal involvement.

Lying

Some parents feel that the lying child undermines the foundation of the parent-child relationship. "We were doing so well and then he lied. It ruined everything. I don't know when to trust him." These parents think that truthfulness is a requirement of a sound parent-child relationship. Without truth from the child, an adult often become extremely hurt or disillusioned. In some homes, getting to the truth with a child becomes a daily mission—a mission impossible. These parents do not have conversations with their AFK child; they have cross examinations.

With many of the behavior problems discussed in this book there is a tendency for parents to see the behavior as a moral issue, or the parent takes the behavior personally. The parent then blames the child and attempts to control the child and his behavior.

So, what do AFK children lie about? They lie about anything and everything. Some will lie about things they've done or haven't done. They lie and deny. They also might exaggerate and try to inflate who they are or what they've done. And, of course, they may lie in an attempt to get others in trouble or to set people against each other. Some AFK kids will untruthfully claim that they've not been abused, while some will allege that they have been victimized when they have not been. Sadly, one AFK mother said, "I assume that everything that comes out of my teenager's mouth is a lie."

Case in Point: JT
Lying

J.T. is a convincing liar. His birth father revealed that even when he threatened to beat J.T. with a belt, the boy would not back down from his ridiculous lies. It was difficult, if not impossible, to disprove J.T.'s fabrications. In the most recent episode, the father caught his son with "the goods." J.T. didn't anticipate his father's early return from work, and when he heard the front door slam, he bolted from the master bedroom, dropping a trail of stolen pocket change as he ran to his room.

CLINICAL INTRODUCTION/CLINICAL SNAPSHOT

Though caught in the act, J.T. again would not recant his lies. He tried three slightly different lies on his father, to no avail; the other boys stole the money; he was just returning the money which the other boys stole; and (in desperation) the money was his – given to him by an unidentified student at school that day. In addition to the lies told to cover stealing, lies similarly appear when J.T. has done something wrong, for example, fought at school, failed to do his homework, etc. When confronted, J.T. lies simply to hide his wrong-doing.

It is not uncommon for the child to actually believe his own lies and distortions of fact. (It may make it easier for the child to stick to the lie and to elaborate on earlier lies with later ones, if he sincerely comes to believe his own untruths.) Children who lie habitually, even when there is no apparent reason to, may have learned a behavior so thoroughly that they almost cannot unlearn it. Even when given encouragement to "fess up," with promises of immunity from punishment, they steadfastly adhere to their stories. Many of these children seem to improve their ability to fabricate and confabulate with age, practice, and parental questioning. At other times, lying serves complicated purposes.

Lying as a reflex to undermine intimacy and trust

Lying may occur when there is not a specific act to conceal. The child has neither stolen nor done something wrong. In these instances, lying emerges out of a reflexive and nearly unconscious need to conceal – not an act, but itself. In these instances, lying acts to spoil intimacy and trust. Lying may serve to keep others at a safe distance from the attachment-disordered foster child who distrusts everyone around him. Lying is just another sign of evasion, withdrawal, and distrust. The child allows nobody in. Lying protects the privacy of his thoughts, feelings, and actions.

Maintains psychological distance from others

Lying provides an excellent way of maintaining psychological distance in relationships with other people. Interestingly, many parents, foster parents, teachers, etc. will tell the deceptive child, "Since you've lied to me in the past, I don't know when I will trust you again." This remark may not be all that punishing for the AFK child who may not want a trust relationship.

Over time the act of lying itself may become rewarding to the child, who gloats secretly over the gullible adult world which believes him.

Lying to avoid punishment

Lying becomes a survival skill in a harshly abusive

home, where the child was beaten even after admitting the truth. Truth-telling is in no way rewarded, and the child's punishment is not softened to reflect the honesty that followed his crime. One fifth grader explained that after admitting to the theft of two cookies, he was beaten by his father who then himself ate the bag of cookies in front of the boy to teach him a lesson.

FORM FOLLOWS FUNCTION
Figuring Out How Lying and Deception Work for the Child

After our usual questioning of when, where, how, how often, and with whom lying occurs, we should have a good picture of the form or structure of a child's lying. Then it's time for us to examine why the child lies.

Nine common reasons (e.g. motives, causes, or purposes) to consider when getting to "why"

1. **ATTENTION:** A child gains and maintains attention, sometimes "negative attention," from interactions with others. *Example: A child lies and is cross examined. Sometimes the parent engages in this grueling grilling for hours or returns to the issue, repeatedly, for days. Or a child may lie and make up stories that draw sympathy from others or that inflate his/her ego.*
2. **ASKING FOR A NEED/WANT TO BE MET:** A youth may be communicating a need or want, though sometimes in a roundabout way. *Example: A child wants people to like him, so he makes up stories to build himself up in their view.*

3. **FEAR OR PHOBIA:** A youth may have an automatic and powerful response to certain triggers or situations. *Example: A child is afraid of being abused if he confesses the truth, so he spins a web of deceit.*

4. **AVOIDING OR ESCAPING:** A youth's behavior may serve to help avoid or escape some undesirable, unpleasant event, task or individual. *Example: A child lies to get out of doing homework.*

5. **REDUCE ANXIETY/PAIN:** May reduce tension or discomfort that the youth feels. *Example: A child may have an automatic reaction to being questioned about anything, even innocuous things. The response may be a knee-jerk lie to help feel safe.*

6. **PROVIDE STIMULATION/PLEASURE:** Some behaviors are fundamentally rewarding and pleasurable. *Example: A child derives some satisfaction from fooling adults. He's good at it; he's a real pro.*

7. **FAMILY ISSUES:** Issues in the family may result in certain behavioral problems in the child. The child may also be modeling behaviors taught by the birthparent. Or, the child may have found that his parents never checked out the truth of his statements, so he never experienced any negative consequences for lying. No one caught him at it. *Example: An AFK adolescent claimed that he was turning in his homework, not thinking that his adoptive mother would stay in contact with his teacher.*

8. **PHYSICAL/MEDICAL:** Physical ailments and psychiatric/neurological disorders can produce certain problem behaviors or symptoms. *Example: A child with a petit mal seizure disorder is "out of contact" and foggy around others much of his day. He makes up lies so as not to appear foolish.*

9. **COGNITIVE DISTORTION:** Some behaviors naturally spring from distortions in the child's thinking or from irrational thoughts. *Example: A child's early experiences have caused him to conclude that it's always better to conceal the truth from adults.* (IBID, page 12)

The emphasis here is that lying can serve the purpose of distancing from others. It can protect the private thoughts, feelings, and actions. Lying helps children who are accustomed to a secret and solitary form of existence. In addition, lying and deception can be protective regarding the fear of abusive punishment. Lying and deception can be a way to engage the caregiver through negative attention-seeking.

AFK FAMILY INTERVENTIONS *for specific lying*
   Lying to distance from others: Understanding that the child is distancing can help the parent reframe the lying and not allow the parent-child relationship to diminish. Offer age or developmental appropriate privacy.
   Fear and self protection: Be aware of your voice, tone, and physical presence when disciplining. Model safety and problem solving. Teach that negotiation, compromise, and listening are more beneficial than lying.

Negatively engaging caregivers: Teach honesty by allowing a change from a dishonest response to an honest response. For example, a child first lies and then admits to hitting his sister. The parent can compliment the courage for truthfulness and yet still needs to consequence the behavior to teach the child additional skills, protect the sister and provide appropriate boundaries.

Falsely inflating self-esteem: Place significant attention on building self esteem in a consistent, targeted way. Make it a point to recognize the youth's accomplishment with interest. Talk about how mistakes and successes are the mixture of life. Amplify strengths.

Lying to exploit others: Be very direct, clear, and focus on holding the youth accountable for the lying. If you are parenting a child that displays this type of lying, it is important to work closely with professionals in order to avoid being drawn into manipulative maneuvering.

Lying is a well established pattern: Respond with "statements of fact." "Statements of fact" present to the child your perception of an event. Why you believe the "statements of fact" is evidence of your perception. Present in a way that is not defensive, but rather fact-based. The parent's utilization of "statements of facts" teaches the child that their lying will be responded to in an honest, direct manner. It will challenge the pattern.

Chapter Four

Differential Diagnosis:

There are a number of diagnoses that can be connected with lying and stealing. Often, lying and stealing can have an impulsive feature which will be reflected in a diagnosis such as ADD/ADHD. Additionally, stubborn insistence or refusal that one has lied, deceived, or stolen will be considered in a diagnosis such as Oppositional Defiant Behavior. When the lying or stealing has a consistent pattern of exploiting or harming others and is connected with illegal activities, the diagnosis of Conduct Disorder will be relevant. Attachment issues are often a basic foundational base to lying and stealing. This sets the psychological stage for the attachment disordered youth to meet their own needs at the expense of others. Additionally, always consider that youth who abuse substances often lie as a way to maintain and conceal their chemically abusive behavior.

It is well documented that many AFK youth are removed from their own families as a result of parental chemical abuse or addiction. Unfortunately, parental chemical usage may not cease with the onset of a pregnancy. As a result, Fetal Alcohol Spectrum Disorders (FASD) may be a dynamic in an AFK youth's emotional/behavioral challenges, including lying and stealing behavior. If parental chemical abuse is present, FASD should always be considered as a factor in assessment, diagnosis, and treatment planning as a reponse to disruptive behaviors such as lying and stealing.

For example, a child with intellectual challenges due to prenatal exposure, may not actually understand that she is a part of the bigger picture. She may have a restricted ability to see that she is responsible for acts that are perceived as lying or stealing. She may report on an event as though she was not there or did not steal it, "I found it" or "I 'just' borrowed it and planned to bring it back". Similarly, learning disabilities should also be considered in assessing the child's ability to understand the dynamics of lying and stealing. Questions regarding the child's ability to comprehend behavior are always important to assess prior to designing interventions.

Additionally, cultural/ethnic influences significantly impact perspectives on sharing, ownership, and shared responsibility for misbehavior. This is a dynamic in cross cultural placements where the AFK parents are of a different culture and/or ethnicity than the AFK youth in the home. It is very important for AFK parents providing cross cultural care to learn about the cultural environment of the youth they are parenting, so that they don't misinterpret behavior that might be normal in a different cultural setting.

PARENTAL RESPONSE *to lying or stealing*

Before leaving this subject a word should be said about "mother's intuition." Typically, it is the AFK mother who has the most powerfully negative feelings towards the child. Professionals only later identify the child as attachment-disordered and by that time, she may already be inaccurately perceived as a cold or rejecting mother. A thorough understanding of the mother's reaction to the child is key to the comprehension of the child's psychopathology. The therapist must listen carefully to the mother's reaction to the child in placement. Subtle, almost invisible communication passes between mother and a child, which may escape the therapist. When mothers suspect that the child's emotions are counterfeit, or when they report feelings of revulsion towards the child, one hypothesis worth considering is that the child makes himself truly repulsive to the mother in some way. Psychotherapists, teachers, caseworkers, friends and neighbors must keep in mind that the child may appear quite different to us. We may have fallen under his spell and be victims of counterfeit emotionality.

When a mother states that affectionate gestures from the child are repugnant to her, the therapist may discover, upon closer examination, that the child's kisses are, in fact, erotic or that his hugs are mechanical. When a mother feels estranged from a child, we may observe that the child demonstrates emotion in shallow and insincere ways: the laugh is too long, too loud, and too forced; the smile is plastered on and reflexive; crying is theatrical and manipulative. Whatever the behavior, the mother is often aware at some level that the relationship between herself and the child is a sham. We must, therefore, weigh her reactions, careful to avoid viewing the problem as hers. When we are fooled by the child, we might align with him and dismiss the mother's reaction.

It is very important for AFK fathers to believe and support their spouse's insight regarding the AFK youth's behavior. Often AFK care is lead by mothers, making her more of a target. A questioning spouse can set the stage for splitting and polarizing between the marital partners. Incorporating AFK fathers into an active parenting process provides a consistent parenting model for the child. In the case of a single parent, consider incorporating other support people such as extended family members or case workers into a role to support the AFK mother.

Final Remarks

Lying and stealing are the great provokers! They can make AFK parents feel exploited and unappreciated. Lying and stealing invite personalization and over-reaction. This distracts from the much needed positive and relational building blocks the parent is trying to lay.

As with all of the AFK youth's behavior challenges, lying and stealing has purpose for the child. Fortunately, with a healthy and supportive AFK home, these behaviors can be reduced or alleviated.

CHAPTER 5

Defiance May Not Be What It Appears To Be

General Introduction/The Big Picture:

If we polled foster parents nationally on the most difficult behaviors in the AFK (Adoptive, Foster, and Kinship) children they've cared for, defiance would probably be in the top three. AFK defiance can seem exaggerated, unrelated to current events, explosive, threatening and confusing. It seems to come and go in an instant and be especially focused on AFK mothers. It can physically and emotionally wear out parents and child welfare workers, and undoubtedly is one of the major reasons disruptions take place in AFK placements.

There are many explanations for defiant behavior.

Defiant behavior can be the result of:
- Child abuse and neglect
- Outgrowth of exposure to insensitive care giving
- Lack of consistent structured love in the past
- Possibly genetic
- A response to primary or secondary childhood trauma
- Manipulation
- A way to emotionally distance

The issue at hand is to understand and impact the AFK child so that their defiance is no longer hurtful to themselves or the people that care about them. Let's look at some possible explanations for defiance and ways to intervene.

There are four kinds of defiance discussed in this chapter:
- Anxious defiance
- Angry defiance
- Patterned defiance
- Defiance in a self-parenting child

Anxious Defiance
Sometimes children and youth are defiant because of strong, overwhelming feelings of anxiety. The defiance is not calculated to drive parents wild; it's not the "rebel without a clue" reflex of adolescents testing out their independence. Anxious defiance has, at its core, a deep apprehension often related to low self-esteem and fear of failure.

Case in Point: Gretchen
Anxious Defiance

Gretchen is an eleven-year-old girl who has been in foster care for approximately nine months. Her father is unknown to her, and her mother is severely drug addicted and living with a suspected physical abuser. Gretchen has contact with her mother through supervised visits. She has two younger half brothers, also in foster care, placed together and residing in the same community. Gretchen sees her brothers at least weekly. Gretchen loves seeing her half brothers and is very protective of them.

Gretchen has done relatively well in foster care. She is a somewhat nonverbal young lady who involves herself marginally with the foster family and often seems preoccupied. She seems most content when she is playing for hours alone at the computer. Recently, she has become increasingly defiant, especially in regards to chore completion, time at the computer, and homework completion. She has also started to talk back to her foster mother, telling her that she doesn't want to do her chores or claiming that she has forgotten to do them. Gretchen can be irritable for days. She has also begun to refuse to go to bed on time. She seems fatigued and possibly depressed. The foster mother thinks that Gretchen is finally showing her "true colors" and that the "honeymoon period" is finally over. The foster mother believes it is important that Gretchen comply with the rules in the home before matters get further out of control. Gretchen's therapist has recommended that Gretchen's computer time be limited and tied to her chore and homework completion.

Gretchen's caseworker has been supervising her visits with her mother. Recently, Gretchen has been questioning her caseworker after the visits whether her mother is using again. Gretchen told her caseworker that she thought that she smelled drugs on her mother and that her mother looked like she was using. She was also concerned about a bruise on her mother's arm. Her mother told her that she had bumped it. Gretchen quizzed her caseworker repeatedly about the condition of her mother following a recent visit.

Gretchen's birth father recently contacted her caseworker. Although never involved, Child Support Enforcement recently located him in an effort to receive payment for Gretchen's foster care expenses. Her father expressed an interest in meeting Gretchen and having her come to live with him with his "new" family several states away. The caseworker initiated a home study process for Gretchen's father through County Social Services in the father's county of residence. When the caseworker told Gretchen about her father's interest, Gretchen's first response was, "What about my brothers and my mother?" Her second comment was, "My mother always said my dad was a bad man."

CLINICAL INTRODUCTION/CLINICAL SNAPSHOT
Anxious Defiance

Gretchen's defiance is probably not based on being oppositional by temperament or character. It may not even be related to the fact that she is in that often pre-adolescent age where hormonal and personality changes are common. Gretchen's history suggests that she is her mother's and brother's caregiver. When children become caregivers too early in their life, they gain a false sense of security in being overly responsible for others. In other words, their own security becomes anchored in taking care of others when they should have been the recipient of care themselves. The child begins to believe their world will not remain secure if they are not in control.

It's highly likely that in Gretchen's case she is discouraged, upset, and perhaps anxious and depressed about her personal assessment of her mother's on-going drug abuse. Although she has not confronted her mother, she verbalized to others that the mother is using drugs again. She is not in a position to supervise her mother or help her overcome the drug problem, so she is stuck where she is in, a foster home, which leaves her feeling helpless.

Additionally, Gretchen's world has recently been rocked by the emergence of her father. She has been told that she may live with her father, who has always been described as a "bad man." She would be leaving her home community where she is close to her half brothers and her mother. She is losing her role as a care giver. The control of her life that she has created is being eliminated and she is not excited about going to live with a birth parent she not only does not know, but whose reputation is negative.

Gretchen's defiance is probably based in anxiety associated with the dramatic changes she may experience. She's angry, but not expressing it to those who perhaps deserve it: her birth mother and father. Instead, the anger is vented toward the foster family.

Gretchen displays common symptoms of anxiety (and clinical depression) like:
- Irritability
- Fatigue
- Preoccupation
- Sleep disturbance[12]

Anxiety Disorders are actually quite common in American children; approximately 1 out of 10 children suffer from them.[13] Because of the added instability in the backgrounds of most AFK (Adoptive, Foster, or Kinship) children, that rate is probably higher in AFK youth. Gretchen's anxieties are specific to anticipated losses, not generalized anxiety.

Anxiety in AFK youth is not limited to children that have been caregivers, but can also be present in youth that have been traumatized through sexual, physical, or emotional neglect. Often these children can be defiant, irritable, hypersensitive, have sleep disturbances and appear pre-occupied.[14]

FORM FOLLOWS FUNCTION
Figuring Out How Anxious Defiance Works for the Child

As we have established in previous chapters, most problem behaviors serve a function. What functions might anxious defiance serve in Gretchen's life?

---

12 American Psychiatric Association, DSM-IV-TR, page 476
13 Family News 2002, Michael G. Conner, Psy.D
14 American Psychiatric Association, DSM-IV-TR, page 468

- She can express fear without appearing vulnerable.
- Anxious defiance is an attempt to maintain control and sameness.
- It is a signal that the AFK child's fear is becoming unmanageable.
- Anxious defiance is a way to always be on the alert for potential harm.
- Anxious definance can be a strategy tool to deal emotionally with the unpredictability of the AFK child's world.
- Anxious defiance is a frightened way to defend oneself.
- Anxious defiance in the foster home is perhaps a safer way to vent emotional upset than direct confrontation of birth parents.

AFK FAMILY INTERVENTIONS
Could it be Anxious Defiance?

Proper Assessment

If anxiety symptoms are interfering with a child's daily functioning, the child should be properly evaluated. The best combination for a good evaluation of a foster child includes:
- Thorough background information provided by the caseworker, AFK parents, the child and if possible, by the child's own parents.
- Psychological tests can help diagnosis the type of anxiety the child is experiencing, and can offer follow-up recommendations for treatment.
- Child psychiatrists are also important in the assessment of anxiety in children, especially if medication is

one of the treatment options. It is essential that AFK parents are included in the follow up recommendations.

Generally, AFK youth that are diagnosed with an anxiety disorder should be referred for therapy services.

AFK parents should be involved in the therapeutic process in order to:
- Recognize how the child's anxiety is affecting them.
- Learn what they can do to support the therapeutic process.
- Provide the therapist with valuable information on how the child is progressing.

Proper assessment responds to the function of anxious defiance by:
- Allowing parents and the child to understand the child's reactions.
- Lessening the child's isolation by creating a team of caring adults.

Redefine defiance as anxiety

If a child's defiance is based in anxiety, parents should not have compliance as their primary goal with the AFK (Adoptive, Foster, or Kinship) child. Too much attention on compliance can escalate the anxious child. This may actually cause the child to push her feelings deeper. Power struggles can too easily become the focus of the child's irritability and distract from the actual causes of the youth's anxiety. This does not mean parents should eliminate structure and expectations for the child. In fact, reasonable specific structure can increase a sense of calm and security for the anxious child. The structure models predictability and control in the home environment. Primary attention should be placed on increasing the foster youth's security in negotiating changes or dealing with the experiences that cause them anxiety. In addition, we need to help Gretchen and other children like her to identify and vocalize their feelings and the reasons for their feelings.

Redefining defiance as anxiety responds to the function of anxious defiance by:
- Removing defiance as a battleground for power struggles between the parent and child.
- Explaining the causes of the anxiety.
- Providing a signal to the AFK parent of what the child is feeling.

Isolate the causes of the anxiety and develop targeted plans

If we break down Gretchen's reasons for becoming recently anxious and defiant, we can develop very specific ways in which to help her deal with her fears. These plans should be constructed with a team, including the foster youth's caseworker, therapist, foster parents, the child and, if appropriate and possible, the child's birth family.

One of Gretchen's primary fears is that she will never live with her birth mother again. A companion fear is the possibility that she may live with her dad. In identifying this possibility as anxiety producing for Gretchen, there are a number of interventions that could be implemented.

Talk with Gretchen. She may need assistance communicating her needs to her mother and stating her fears about living with her father. Gretchen may be terrified and silenced by the fear that if she confronts her mother, her mother will stop visits. Gretchen may need help expressing her frustration about her half-brothers being able to return to live with her mother while she cannot. In any case, these fears would be the guide for designing steps that could help Gretchen in approach this transition with less anxiety.

It would be important to repeatedly explain to Gretchen that there would be a number of steps that would take place before any decision could be made on Gretchen's possible move. How much control Gretchen will have regarding any decision must be clearly identified to her. The team may decide that moving Gretchen to her birth father's home may not be in her best interest.

If it appears that Gretchen's father may be a parental option for her, request that he begin the process of making contact with Gretchen in a slow, safe manner. This could be through the exchange of letters, pictures of himself, his family, a video tape showing his current home and neighborhood. She would then have ample time to think it through, question, and talk about her feelings with her support network. Moving in a slow, structured manner is the smartest way to handle life transitions for anxious foster youth.

Isolating the causes of anxious defiance and developing targeted plans responds to the function of anxious defiance by:
- Assisting the AFK parents and child with an understanding of the child's reactions, which were once confusing.
- Creating a team of caring adults to lessen the youth's feelings of isolation.
- Providing an opportunity for the youth to learn that life is not simply governed by being in or out of control.

What if the child is not an anxious youth, but more defiant than what is considered developmentally normal and realistic? There are other reasons that an AFK youth may be defiant.

Angry Defiance

Many AFK youth use angry defiance as a way not to connect with their AFK parents. This can operate on both a conscience and unconscious level. Unfortunately, many AFK youth have experienced adults and parents as threatening and dangerous. This doesn't mean a child doesn't love his/her birth family. However, if the child has experienced the misuse of anger in their home we know that defiance, and all too often violence, has been modeled as an acceptable manner in handling emotions in relationships. It has also been modeled as a way to control others and fulfill one's needs. The AFK child brings this experience into their AFK home and is well-trained in how not to connect with adults, regardless of the adult's intentions.

Case in Point: Jenny
Angry Defiance

Jenny is a fourteen-year-old female currently residing in treatment foster care. She has been in foster care on four previous occasions beginning at age three. She was reunified all three times with her birth mother and her younger sister. Jenny is frustrated that her sister can remain at home and she cannot. Jenny has some juvenile legal difficulties and cannot be placed in the birth home. There have been a variety of "live-in" boyfriends in the family as well. Jenny's birth father's whereabouts are unknown.

Jenny's birth family has previously used a variety of services. They have been involved in intensive in-home therapy, juvenile services case management, and tracking services for school truancy. Jenny's mother suffers from depression, addiction issues and has been involved in a number of violent, exploitative relationships. Jenny is not seeing a therapist now because she refuses to participate. There are suspicions that Jenny has been sexually abused, but the allegations have never been substantiated.

Jenny maintains an angry distance in the foster home. She refuses to engage with the foster family. She is silently disapproving and is an expert at manipulating curfews, chores and communications into detailed battles with the foster parents. When Jenny is called on her behavior, she denies it and isolates herself afterward. Jenny does not verbally challenge her foster father but can become verbally abusive to her foster mother when the foster father is not present. When asked about her goals, Jenny says she wants to get out of foster care so that she can be with her friends and family.

Chapter Five

CLINICAL INTRODUCTION/CLINICAL SNAPSHOT
Angry Defiance

Many times angry defiance can seem vengeful and nonsensical to the AFK parent. Jenny's behavior of arguing and opposing her foster mother over the simplest request is an excellent example. Another example is the child who pleasantly agrees with the parent's request and yet fails to follow through time after time.

A function of both of these behaviors is that the youth remains in control by consistently frustrating and disappointing the parents through opposing them, or by not following through. This is often a more appealing option for the child because there is little risk of connecting and possibly compromising their loyalty to their birth family. Additionally, AFK parents, especially AFK mothers, become targets for the child's angry defiance. Interestingly, Jenny may have learned a pattern in the past of keeping her birth mother involved through negative, defiant behaviors. It may have been part of her role as scapegoat in a family where her sister was the clear favorite. Jenny may have imported that role into the foster family. It's a role that sends unclear signals to the family: leave me alone-watch me like a hawk. Stay away—stay close. This is the dilemma.

The dilemma in parenting a child that is angrily defiant is they are constantly inviting you to over-parent them. As the angrily defiant child pushes away, the AFK parent creates a situation where the parent feels the need to correct, consequence, and at times, overreact. This "over-parenting" almost always creates a situation where the child successfully pulls off a "gotcha," leaving the parent frustrated and disappointed.

FORM FOLLOWS FUNCTION
Figuring Out How Angry Defiance Works for the Child:

- Angry defiance allows the AFK child to maintain or re-establish control.
- Angry defiance is a way for the child to maintain a safe distance from caregivers—stay close—stay away!
- Angry defiance is a way for the child to act out feelings of revenge towards the AFK parents.
- Angry defiance is a way for the AFK child to separate from "over-parenting."
- Angry defiance can be a way to recreate their birth home experiences.

AFK FAMILY INTERVENTIONS *for Angry Defiance*

Don't over-parent and/or over-engage

Angry defiant youth are often experts at engaging the AFK parents in reacting to their defiance. Reacting to defiance often leads to over-reacting, which sets up situations where the parent often disciplines in ways they may regret and models inconsistency. When a parent is inconsistent, the parent loses credibility and reinforces defiance as an effective way to undermine the parent. Work to keep battles with the AFK child at a minimum. Reframe these as invitations to engage the child. Often, decisions on consequences can be pre-planned or applied after the incident has calmed. Parents need to know what behaviors "push their buttons," so that the child has a more difficult time engaging the parent negatively. Try preemptive approaches of positive, if titrated, doses of parental attention.

By not over-parenting and/or over-engaging, the AFK parent is responding to the function of angry defiance by:

- Not reinforcing an unhealthy way for the AFK child to remain in control.
- Allowing the AFK child to maintain a safe distance without conflict.
- Not re-enacting an unhealthy relationship pattern that the child has experienced.
- Eliminating an opportunity for revenge based behavior.

Have a well thoughtout safety plan

Generally, a youth that is experiencing difficulties with defiance has other people involved in their care. This may include a child welfare social worker, a therapist, juvenile authorities, school personnel, etc. Involve these parties in constructing a safety plan for the child. *Using Jenny as an example, two steps in the safety plan could be:*

- **Identify calming and distancing techniques** to use in approaching Jenny when she is escalating and defiant.
    Examples:
    1. *Redirect her.*
    2. *Create physical and emotionall distance from Jenny.*
    3. *Verbally reinforce any behavior that is not defiant and indicates Jenny's willingness to re-involve herself in the routine of the family.*

- **Learn what Jenny's signs are** when she is feeling defiant.
  Examples:
  1. *Look for cues regarding Jenny's mood,*
  2. *Study how she engages (arguing, exiting)*
  3. *Look for signs of fatigue, injury, illness.*
  4. *"Red flag" events that are stressful for Jenny and how she reacts to them.*

Safety plans should include what the AFK parent's need in order to maintain their emotional health in caring for her. Since Jenny is in foster care, these supports could include:

- Respite
- Child welfare worker response
- Mentor foster family
- Planned debriefing with the child welfare worker and/or the therapist regarding episodes of defiance.

Any successful safety plan is dependent on the AFK (Adoptive, Foster, or Kinship) parents feeling comfortable and supported in being able to follow through the steps in the plan.

Having a well thought out safety plan responds to the function of angry defiance by:

- Modeling for the child that adults can respond to them in a consistent, supportive manner even when they are feeling defiant.
- Not allowing the child to control a situation in an unhealthy manner.

- Positioning the parent to have pre-planned and supported ways to respond to defiance.
- Respecting the child's need for distance and separateness in situations that are stressful for the child.

Patterned Defiance

Sometimes defiance is related to a long-standing, ever-building process that's been occurring in the parent-child relationship. Although it's possible for the defiance to look like it appeared overnight, under the microscope you can usually detect the process. One common form of patterned defiance is found in families where a child is extremely impulsive, shows poor judgment, cannot regulate his behavior, and acts hyperactively. Commonly, this child is diagnosed with ADD or ADHD. Over time, the child seems to evolve into an increasingly defiant family member.

Case in Point: Robert
Patterned Defiance

Robert has been a handful his whole life. His grandmother, who has raised him on-and-off over the youth's 14 years, is exhausted. An only child of a neglectful mother, Robert was left with grandmother periodically when the mother disappeared because of drug abuse problems.

Even as a tot, Robert has always "had the motor running," according to his grandmother, a gentle, non-directive woman. "He was always dashing here or jumping on top of things, or climbing the fence out of my back yard. I had to stay on him all the time. It was an exhausting time in my life." Though Robert has slowed down some over the years, he has continued to be a handful. According to the grandmother, around the age of 11, he became more "mouthy." She says he argues about everything and defies her rules. He lives with her full-time now, and she still can't get him to settle down.

CLINICAL INTRODUCTION/CLINICAL SNAPSHOT
Patterned Defiance

In Robert's case, we see the evolution of a child who likely was exhibiting signs of ADHD earlier in his life. His behavior in a way coerced his grandmother to be a super parent, one who had to be on him constantly for safety's sake. Since he was so impulsive and out-of-control, she increased her own control. In a word, she over-regulated young Robert. Overregulation of ADHD children has been found to correlate to more parent-child conflict, e.g.; Parent: "Get down from that rooftop!" Child: "Make me!"

In any case, it's typical for parents to find themselves using more directions, more external controls, and more anger when they are raising children who don't control their impulses well and are hyperactive on top of it. The parent gradually becomes more intrusive. Out of an exasperated shotgun approach, the parent tries a range of management approaches including commands, repeated commands, threats, repeated threats, physical discipline, multiple reminders, and sometimes, ignoring and withdrawal. The nature of the parent-child relationship becomes increasingly negative and conflicted. It's a war zone. The parent seeks compliance and obedience along with a semblance of good behavior. The child fights it tooth and nail. After years of struggle, the relationship can deteriorate to the point where the parent either pulls back and withdraws from the battle or seemingly overreacts out of pure exasperation. (Or, the parent may vacillate between the two approaches: withdraw for a while; explode; withdraw for another while; explode; wash-rinse-repeat!)

FORM FOLLOWS FUNCTION
How Patterned Defiance Works for the Child:
- It engages a parent in a familiar struggle.
- It allows the child to vent frustration.
- It is an attempt by the child to carve out some independence and autonomy.

AFK FAMILY INTERVENTIONS *for Patterned Defiance*

Prove patterned defiance is ineffective

Many AFK youth have had numerous "success experiences" where their patterned defiance has caused caregivers to give-in or give-up. As a result of these successes, defiance moves from being a periodic response to a patterned way of interacting with caregivers. The caregiver begins to feel frustrated and exhausted.

The first step in changing patterned defiance is to quit allowing it to work. This sounds simple, but the youth that has mastered patterned defiance, has a "sixth sense" of when the parent is frustrated, exhausted, or ready to over-react. The first step in proving that defiant behavior is ineffective begins with the foster parent becoming aware of his/her own reactions to the challenges of patterned defiance, and responding differently. Be aware, the AFK child that has mastered the use of patterned defiance will fight to continue its success!

Proving pattern defiance ineffective responds to the functions of patterned defiance by:
- Modeling for the child that the AFK parent is in control of their reactions.
- Not supporting patterned defiance as an effective way to problem solve in relationships.

Pre-plan routines and consequences

Unfortunately, many AFK youth have experienced families as reactive and chaotic. Previous caregivers may have been unable to provide healthy routines for the AFK youth, and this supports patterned defiance working for the youth. Routines are important for children as they teach the child a sense of order and provide them with an "outline" of how relationships and the "larger" world work. For the AFK youth that has not received consistency in their life, routines initially can be misinterpreted as attempting to control the child and can become a battleground for resistance. Having a routine for a child, if provided consistently and positively, can eventually become reassuring for the child and provide them with an opportunity to be successful. The same perspective applies to consequences for positive and negative behavior. Initially, consequences are almost always met with resistance, but youth generally will accept them provided that they are:
- balanced both negatively and positively.
- not reactively applied.
- communicated ahead of time as much as possible.

Pre-planning routines and consequences responds to the functions of patterned defiance by:
- Establishing predictability and allowing the parent to respond to the child's challenges in a planned, nonreactive manner.
- Providing the parents with a plan for responding to the challenges of patterned defiance.

Defiance of a Self-Parented Child

Defiance can be seen in the self-parented child who is totally unfamiliar with being too parented or disciplined and has virtually raised himself by his own rules. This child has often been sorely neglected, frequently abandoned, and left to his or her own devices. Without an adult to turn to or be accountable to, the child becomes his own boss. He is the master of his destiny, and it's shocking or maddening to him to encounter adults who attempt to control or guide him.

Case in Point: Morgan
Defiance of a Self-Parented Child

Morgan is an unkempt pre-teenaged girl who was found dumpster diving in the downtown area of a large city. When driven to her home, no sign of any adult was found. Morgan seemed vague about the whereabouts of her mother, but was comfortable being left home alone. Since no adult could be located, Morgan was placed in emergency foster care.

In the foster home several days later, the foster mother reported that Morgan was self-sufficient and bucked any authority figures. She will glare wordlessly when given parental directives. She will stomp off to her room if she is not allowed to "run the household, cook, clean and boss the other kids around," according to the foster mother.

CLINICAL INTRODUCTION/CLINICAL SNAPSHOT

Some foster and adopted children have come from backgrounds without viable parent figures to guide them. Neglect is rampant. Parent absence—both physical and emotional—is typical. Essentially, the children raise themselves and become feral. Limits, rules, structure, and guidance simply do not exist. The parent vacuum is filled by the child's own efforts, survival instincts, and needs. Left to his own devices, he does not seek out parent figures for support, nurturance, or structure. In other words, he is a self-parenting child.

Once feral, self-parenting children are taken into foster care, there is a huge culture shock, a collision of worlds. The child has his familiar world of loneliness and rugged individualism and the foster parents have theirs, typically a world in which children respond to parents. And, here's the collision in a nutshell; the child has no inherent desire to respond to the parents. That's Greek to him. The parents ask for the usual, "We set the rules. Our children comply," and it doesn't work. The child bucks and fights the discipline and structure parents try to offer. And, voila, we have a child who is defiant and oppositional.

FORM FOLLOWS FUNCTION
Figuring Out How Defiant, Self-Parenting Works for the AFK Child

- The child continues to be independent without adult input or intervention.
- No risk of depending on and trusting adults.
- The child remains in control of meeting his/her own needs in a way he/she has found to be successful.

AFK FAMILY INTERVENTIONS
for Defiance and Self-Parenting

Allow the AFK child to remain in control of specific areas of his/her life that are safe for the child.

Parents often believe that an AFK child needs to respect and comply with all of the rules and structure of their "new" home. Self-parented children seldom comply with this belief. Instead, they will resist, defy, and fight to remain in control of meeting their own needs. Generally, youth like this have been self-parenting for a long time; probably from infancy. As a result, this pattern is usually well established and difficult to change. To the self-parented child, their way of managing the world has worked for them, no matter how distorted this may appear to adults.

A common area in which a self-parented child will fight to remain in control is when he/she has "parented" younger siblings. The self-parented child, who is often referred to as parentified, will refuse and often undermine the AFK parent's appropriate efforts to create a family and parent. Instead of trying to wrestle control from the self-parented child, try sharing and respecting the relationship with the self-parented child. While "sharing" the parenting, the AFK parent should consistently reinforce the message that the siblings will be OK with other's parenting. Additionally, the parent should reinforce the self-parented child being more involved as a sibling than as a parent.

Allowing the self-parented child to remain in control, in safe areas, responds to the function of defiance and the self-parented child by:
- Modeling for the child that the AFK parents can respect areas that the self-parented child has identified as important and has displayed skills.
- Not allowing the relationship between the AFK child and parent to become a repetitive power struggle.

Teach negotiation; reinforce all efforts by the self-parented child to work cooperatively

The self-parenting child often enters an AFK placement with little ability to negotiate relationships. They have not experienced adults that can parent in a manner that reinforces cooperation. All too often, caregivers in their lives have been the dispensers of trauma, which the self-parented child then generalizes to all adults. They may have adjusted by developing the ability to "wear-out" adults through their defiance and, at other times, they are able to fake cooperation until they learn the vulnerable areas of the AFK parent.

It is important for parents to verbally highlight and reinforce for the self-parented child how cooperation works. For example, if the self-parented child refuses to complete a required task, the child should be given a consequence for non-compliance. After the consequence has been given and the tension has subsided, the parents should review the child's choices and assess consequences for future non-compliance.

Defiant, self-parented children usually view conflicts with parents as either win or lose situations. The idea of choices and options in relationships are often foreign.

Teaching and reinforcing cooperation responds to the function of the defiant self-parented child by:
- Providing the child with replacement skills other than relying on defiance.
- Positioning the AFK parent to support the child's growth rather than locking into a cycle of giving-in or reacting.

Differential Diagnosis:

There are a number of reasons that AFK youth may display defiance. It is important that the parent look for the functions of the defiance before reacting to what appears to be challenges to the authority of the parent. In considering the four functions of defiant behavior, the following psychiatric conditions or diagnoses could be present.

Gretchen – Anxious Defiance
- Anxiety Disorders
- Depression Disorders

Jenny – Angry Defiance
- Oppositional Defiant Disorder (ODD)
- Mood Disorder

- Disruptive Behavior Disorder
- Depressive Disorder
- Attachment Disorder

Robert – Patterned Defiance
- ADD
- ADHD
- Oppositional Defiant Disorder (ODD)

Morgan – Defiance of A Self-Parented Child
- Attachment Disorder
- Oppositional Defiant Disorder
- Anxiety Disorder
- Depression disorders

PARENTAL RESPONSE *to defiance*

Defiance can cause AFK parents to over-react, over-punish, feel exhausted, and create self-questioning in their parenting abilities. Defiance generally does not create parental empathy for the AFK child but it can create feelings in the parent of wanting to give-up and surrender.

What defiant AFK youth need most is what their defiance erodes. The child needs a response from the parent that is not personalized or reactive. In the four defiance scenarios of this chapter, all are the result of the AFK youth having incorporated defiance as a way to try to control their world. Unfortunately, defiance has worked for the children in a maladaptive way.

Although the scenarios presented differ according to function, they all have similar strategies for the AFK parent to consider.

These strategies include:
- Look for the purpose of the defiance.
- Protect yourself against personalization of the defiance.
- Identify ways to teach and support the AFK youth in replacing defiance.
- Establish boundaries and consequences for defiance that are inappropriate.

Final Remarks:

The backgrounds of youth in AFK care are a blueprint in how to develop a defiant response to life's challenges. Without significant adults to teach, nurture, correct and support their negotiation of life, defiance has emerged as an effective function for the child to control their emotional response to relationships and external challenges. Simply put, parental neglect, and all too often abuse, has denied the child the ability to self-regulate emotionally and behaviorally. It would be naive to think that all degrees of defiance could be treated and responded to in a family and community setting. However, we remain committed to the belief that if at all possible, defiant youth can be best taught, supported, and cared for in AFK care. Support for the parent is important when dealing with the overwhelming demands of a defiant AFK child. Often a mental health therapist that is skilled, and has an understanding of the dynamics of AFK care, can be helpful in working with the child and parents.

CHAPTER 6

Naughty, Naughty: Relentless Negative Behaviors

General Introduction/The Big Picture:

Many foster and adoptive parents lament that they hate the relationship they have developed with a particular child in their home. A long list of problem behaviors haunts their dreams. "I'm always the disciplinarian with this child. I spend so much time riding this child for his bad behavior that I don't like the child or even have the energy to be positive with the child." This child is an enormous drain on the AFK parent. It may be found that there is no one single overriding concern that the parents have. Instead, they struggle against the chronic pile-up of lots of little problems. The parent feels they are not allowed to be the parent they'd like to be to this child.

There's no limit on how many problem behaviors a child can have. Some kids don't present their parents with one or two problem behaviors; they have a multitude. Or, they show such a variety of negative behaviors that it's not enough to focus on a stand-out behavior, you need to address all of them. Negative behaviors provide the ultimate tool for engaging parents and others, e.g., teachers, other children, etc. An interesting book by the National Association of Special Education teachers describes the negative attention phenomenon this way:

Some students misbehave to try to attract teacher attention. Surprisingly, many students who value adult attention don't really care if it is positive (praise) or negative attention (reprimands)—they just want attention! [15]

AFK (Adoptive, Foster, or Kinship) parents also get drawn into the "reprimand" trap.

Listen to one such parent

This child drains me with naughty behavior of one kind or a variety of behaviors. I'm always on this child. I have to spend more time correcting and punishing this child than all my other children combined. She argues with me; she disobeys but always gets caught; she is "accident-prone", maybe on purpose; and she takes up all my time. I get the feeling that she prefers being in trouble and doesn't feel comfortable being a good girl. Oh, and she is a bottomless pit of needs. She is sneaky but always gets caught. It keeps me acting like a police man. With her, it's not one big thing; it's every little thing going wrong constantly.

---

15 (http://www.naset.org)

Case in Point: Carson

Carson was in solitary confinement—again. It was a common occurrence. Carson, age seven, violated a rule and was paying the price. Oddly, he seemed unbothered and even mildly pleased. When his adoptive father barked at him, he grinned a "Gotcha" smirk. This infuriated his father even further.

The adoptive mother identified several of Carson's behaviors. He has temper tantrums, fights with his brother, bed wets, steals items around the house, and lies. "Last night," she reported wearily, "I put Carson in time out 20-30 times. My whole evening was consumed with Carson."

CLINICAL INTRODUCTION/CLINICAL SNAPSHOT

Evolution of problem behaviors over time can suggest that the child's negative behaviors can be eliminated one-by-one, but something else keeps cropping up. Carson had begun with stealing, which really was a continuation of a behavior he had used to help him survive in a neglectful early life prior to adoption. At first, his adoptive parents were understandably concerned, but the problem seemed to abate over time. The problem disappeared and Carson still seemed very needy but not naughty, until the arrival of the parents' birth child.

FORM FOLLOWS FUNCTION
Figuring Out How Constant Negative Behavior Works for the Child

Negative behavior is a problem that is somewhat shapeless and yet ubiquitous. It's everywhere all the time and it morphs, if it must. We get a handle on the stealing and then sibling rivalry comes to the front. The sibling rivalry recedes and here comes lying. Lying disappears and the child starts to act out with self-harm. As with all problem behaviors, it's important to understand the function or purpose of the conduct problem.

After pinpointing the structure of the problem by asking the important questions (i.e., what, when, where, how, how often, and with whom,) we then collect information on function.

Here again are nine common reasons, causes, functions, motives or purposes:

1. **ATTENTION:** A youth gains and maintains attention, sometimes "negative attention," from interactions with others.

2. **ASKING FOR A NEED/WANT TO BE MET:** A youth may be communicating a need or want, though sometimes in a roundabout, provocative, and non-verbal way.

3. **FEAR OR PHOBIA:** A youth may have an automatic and powerful response to certain triggers or situations. A child may find positive attention, warmth and nurturance to be foreign and frightening. Negative attention is more familiar and, oddly, acceptable.

4. **AVOIDING OR ESCAPING:** A youth's misbehavior may serve to help avoid or escape some undesirable,

unpleasant event, task or individual. Negative attention gets him out of doing things or going places when he's uncomfortable.

5. **REDUCE ANXIETY/PAIN:** May reduce tension or discomfort that a youth feels. Some children, if not the constant center of attention, feel invisible, worthless, and abandoned.

6. **PROVIDE STIMULATION/PLEASURE:** Some behaviors are fundamentally rewarding and pleasurable. Coercing attention from others with misbehavior or watching them respond to mischief or misbehavior may be enjoyable.

7. **FAMILY ISSUES:** Issues in the family may result in certain behavior and behavior problems in a youth. For instance, a needy child may feel his position is usurped by the arrival of another child.

8. **PHYSICAL/MEDICAL:** Physical ailments and psychiatric/neurological disorders can produce certain problem behaviors or symptoms. For instance, children with A.D.H.D. can become part of an increasingly negative parent-child relationship where the parent must always over-regulate them for impulsive behavior. The child grows used to the familiar negative parent-child relationship.

9. **COGNITIVE DISTORTION:** Some behaviors naturally spring from distortions in a youth's thinking or

from irrational thoughts. For example, the child's early experiences may have caused him to conclude that if he doesn't force the caregivers to attend to him, they will forget him. (IBID, page 12)

Many forms of conduct problem have in common an underlying function, which is to keep the parent engaged with the child. In many AFK children and teenagers the most common purpose of constant, negative behavior is attention. Their negative behavior coerces parents to stay riveted to him, engaged with him, and tangled up in a negative pattern. The child's behavior does the talking for him. If the purpose is to achieve attention, the behavior screams; "Watch me, see me, interact with me, me, me!" The function is to keep the parent involved, to keep this child on center stage. Another function is to punish the parent for straying from the mission.

Children like these often drop their negative behaviors and are quieted by the "4 U's" — undivided, undiluted, uninterrupted, and unending attention. Parents report, "Oh, sure, as long as we are—just the two of us—shopping, or riding in the car singing a song, things are bliss; she is a totally different creature." If the child receives one-to-one attention, he/she seem to do spectacularly well. If that blissful relationship is disrupted in any way, the negative attention-seeking begins again. We're back to the naughty child.

A second finding is that these children seem inarticulate and verbally passive when it comes to making their needs known. If they are compared with age mates or with their healthier siblings, we often find that they are strangely silent about their feelings and needs. They don't clamor for attention as much as they extort it with behavior problems. Sadly, children with maltreatment backgrounds have failed to distinguish between positive and negative attention. They'll settle for either. In fact, the child may over time grow to prefer negative attention, because it has become so familiar to them.

In summary, negative attention-seeking behavior has as its primary functions:

- To gain the attention of the AFK parents at all costs.
- To maintain the parent's attention through a system that has proven successful for the child.
- To provide the child with an indirect way to punish or release negative emotions projected unto AFK parent.

AFK FAMILY INTERVENTIONS
Learn to Track and Identify

It's important to focus upon when, where, how, how often, and with whom the problem behaviors occur. Identify which of the behaviors is most frustrating and disrupts family life the most. If you focus upon all the behaviors at once, it can be too daunting a task for parent and child. Try to help the parents zero in on a problem behavior that occurs frequently, as in daily or hourly.

Importantly, we must focus the parents' gaze upon what is missing. The behavior problems are obvious, and often, in-your-face in intensity. They aren't hard to pinpoint. Parents must look past the obvious behavior to see what is missing.

Ask the parents how often the child verbalizes needs, wants, and feelings to look for patterns.

Inquire about the child's capacity to voice needs or dissatisfactions. Ask them if he is assertive and forthcoming with them about what he wants from them, about how others get more than him, about the issue of fairness, etc.

One way to address this quickly is to ask parents to identify the most honest, pushy, candid, and "never-take-no-for-an-answer" child in the home. Usually parents can easily name a child or two who "reaches for the brass ring." This child has a mind of his own and is not shy about sharing it. He is a frequent visitor to the complaint department. He tries verbally to convince the parents of his needs, and he shares his desires and wants frequently and clearly. He is influential, and feels effective and confident about explaining his position in words to his parents. And, he fully expects to walk way from encounters with some modicum of what he needs. This is the gold standard child against which the parents should be comparing the naughty, negative attention-seeking child.

For this reason, it is important to establish what we call "the gold standard child." Parents need to identify the child in their home who complains, protests, begs, pleads, harangues, pesters, disagrees, and presses unrelentingly for the meeting of his her felt needs at the moment. If they compare that child's volume and quality of complaining to that of the naughty child, the stark differences appear. The naughty child frequently exhibits small amounts of pestering and pleading. The child does not use the strength of words to get needs met within the relationship with the parent. Instead, the child uses behavior to extort attention and to influence the parent's behavior. Naughty behavior is a potent force and it develops into a "lose-lose" environment in the home.

AFK FAMILY INTERVENTIONS
Learn About The Function

It's important to identify what is missing when encountering negative attention-seeking behavior. You want good behavior; the child wants you. You are seeking two different goals. Her behavior is doing the talking for her and expressing her feelings and desires.

Generally, the AFK child has always felt deprived and unloved. "That's not fair." She is not using protest and outcry, but rather negatively engages the parent to respond to her need for attention and parental involvement.

Often, traditional behavioral interventions such as putting her on a regimen of a point or level system may keep her permanently locked into the bottom. Parents often find that they have run out of consequences, further frustrating them, and leaving them feeling ineffective.

Interestingly, the parents find that the AFK child might talk when getting a personal shampoo. She'll even talk about her day at school, if given one-to-one time. This leaves the AFK parent confused. Why can't we have more of these discussions? The parent doesn't understand why they can't positively interact with the child more frequently.

Coming up with Interventions

Carve out some one to one time. Bedtime can be a wonderful time with younger children to reinforce the positive behavior, and the connection the parent feels for the child.

With the older child, you could initiate communication of your positive feelings for the child; take the lead in expressing both your wish to connect with the youth and also your commitment to them and their best interests.

Encourage your child to request attention in words several times daily. Look for what's missing, routinely voicing the need for help from, or time with, you. If the child does not ask frequently enough in a positive fashion, remind the child to make a request and coach the child to speak up.

Using the information you have gained from tracking the negative attention-seeking behavior, try to use "preemptive strikes" of positive attention. If the child's pattern is to engage you negatively once per hour, try to match the frequency with hourly positive attention. It's important to jump the gun on the child by providing "random positive attention" before the child demands his hourly dose of negativity.

A different approach to behavioral interventions could be posting "green cards" on a bulletin board. Have her vigilantly watch the bulletin board for times when you are available (green) for attention.

Have her use chits for attention. Five cards per day, for instance, that allow her to initiate in a game-like fashion. Get her to request attention as needed.

Differential Diagnosis:

As with so many AFK youth's behavioral and emotional challenges, early damaged attachments with caregivers, most often initiated by childhood abuse and neglect, set the stage for youth to seek attention in a negative way. Their bids for positive attention probably went unnoticed, but negative, troublesome bids would get the results they were seeking; extra attention! As a result, the stage has been set for a negative working model in seeking parental nurturance. The other "D" diagnoses will show themselves in negative attention-seeking behavior (ADD, ADHD, ODD). The primary feature, whether it is in large or small doses, is the lack of consistent, positive attachments with caregivers.

Final Remarks:

Don't give up! Recognize that a child can be re-directed and influenced into seeking attention in positive ways. However, remember that old habits are hard to break. Parents must "pre-think" times to show and teach the child the reciprocity of positive exchanges. Look at it from the perspective that positive parental input must "out score" negative parental input before the game changes. Teaching the child to protest is essential in order for the child to learn that legitimate needs can be met through directly expressing them to the AFK parent.

CHAPTER 7

The Wisdom of the Experts: What AFK Youth and AFK Families Have Taught Us

General Introduction/The Big Picture:

In our professional careers, we have had the opportunity to work with, and maintain relationships with a number of AFK youth and their AFK families on a long term basis. As these youth have matured, adjusted to stability, and healed many of the emotional wounds of their early years, they have been able to understand and explain some of the functions of their adaptive yet baffling behaviors. The learning and inspiration that they have given us through their stories is simply remarkable. A number of the stories in this chapter are from youth that are now adults and who have reflected back on their behavior and foster care experience. The remainder of the stories focus on creative interventions that have helped and supported AFK youth as they've responded to difficult situations, often represented through complex behaviors. In order to protect confidentiality, changes have been made to youth demographics, case dynamics and processes that might be identifiable factors.

FUNCTION:
Protecting Myself From Potentially Hurtful Adults

Jeremy was fifteen when he arrived at his fourth foster care home. He entered this foster home upon discharge from his most recent residential placement. Jeremy's previous foster placement lasted nine days, and disrupted after he ran away, stole from his foster parents, and threatened them with violence. Jeremy had been in a number of institutional care settings, which included a highly structured psychiatric hospital, a residential facility and two juvenile correctional facilities. He did well in all of those institutional placements and rapidly rose through the behavioral levels with ease. He formed good relationships with the majority of the staff and quickly established himself as a positive leader among his peers in all of his institutional placements.

Jeremy's original removal from his home was because of extreme physical and sexual abuse. He was never reunified with his family because of the severity of the physical and sexual abuse. Parental rights were terminated and he entered the child welfare and juvenile correction systems of care at age eleven.

Jeremy maintained the foster care placement he entered at age fifteen until he graduated from high school. Now close to age thirty, Jeremy still identifies his last foster family as his permanent family, which is welcomed by the foster family. So why did this placement work?

Talking with Jeremy, he clearly articulates the reasons why his last foster care placement worked. For Jeremy, having a foster placement succeed was all about perceiving the adults that cared for him as being safe. Jeremy had experienced safety in his institutional placements. While in institutional care, he felt safe as he came to trust many of the child care staff with whom he worked. They both protected him and cared about him. Additionally, all of the expectations in the institution were clear and predictable. School was individualized, recreation options were available and Jeremy was successful and felt positive about himself in the context of these institutional settings.

When Jeremy was discharged to his fourth foster home at age fifteen, he went to a home that was experienced and not reactive to many of the challenges foster youth can present. The foster parents began the placement by giving him a tour of their home. The tour not only included showing Jeremy his room, but also incorporated into the tour were explanations on family rules regarding food, where the family had conversations, alone time, use of the bathroom, locking doors both inside and outside. What caught Jeremy's attention was the emphasis on his safety, even though the foster parents probably did not emphasize this intentionally. Jeremy vividly remembers how they explained to him that he could lock the bathroom door when he used it to guarantee privacy. The foster parents assured him that they had a key to the bathroom, but would only use it in times of emergency. Slowly, Jeremy decided to risk trusting the foster parents and decided to give the placement a chance. He knew he could always use defiance, stealing, and threats of violence as a manner by which to return to institutional care. Luckily, he did accept the caring, structure, and concern his new foster parents showed him. But as Jeremy reiterated, it all began with him feeling safe outside of an institutional setting.

FUNCTION:
I Want to be with People That Look Like Me

I once worked for a foster care organization that had as a part of their services a higher education scholarship program. I had the good fortune to be the case manager of a young lady, Betsy, who was of a mixed ethnic background. She was primarily African American, which is how the world identified her. Betsy had been in a long term foster care placement with a Caucasian family. She was very connected to her foster family, did well in school and had numerous long term friendships in the community where she spent the majority of her growing up years. The community was primarily Caucasian with no one of African American heritage residing in the community. Unfortunately, Betsy's biological family was not a reliable source of support for her.

As we planned for college, I strongly suggested that Betsy stay close to her support systems. She had big plans and wanted to study in a college that was further from her support systems. She finally agreed to attend a local college. During the first year of college, Betsy did low-average work academically and did not express much motivation or interest in her studies or college activities.

Helping professionals are excellent at speculating at why situations are not going as expected. I speculated that Betsy was having transition difficulties and that leaving the foster home had pushed a number of emotional issues forward. I also considered that Betsy might be abusing chemicals or could be depressed. I attempted to discuss these issues with Betsy but got little confirmation from her that they were significant. She reiterated that she still wanted to attend a larger college, in a larger city. She had a college selected, and we visited it. Betsy was excited after the campus tour and desperately wanted to transfer. I hesitantly supported her decision.

As Betsy's first semester progressed at the new college, she continued to report enthusiasm for her course work, her new friends, classes, and the community in which the college was located. This remained consistent into her junior year, her senior year and carried through her graduation. As I reflected back with Betsy on why this particular college worked for her, she taught me a number of lessons. She said that although she loved her foster family, she realized that her life would be very different from theirs and one of the reasons was because of race. Being supported and cared for by her foster family was not enough and that she needed to be with, and learn about, people that "looked like her." At her second college, for the first time in her life, she experienced being with a group of African Americans in her own age group. It was a very special moment for her and yet somewhat confusing. Many of the nuances of African American culture were unknown to her, and it was noticed by some of the African American students. They were generally very accepting and embracing of her background, and helped ease her discomfort. These relationships allowed Betsy to experience a world that she was unable to experience as a foster child in a Caucasian home, in a dominantly Caucasian community.

Betsy is currently in her early thirties. She is successful, respected in her profession and incredibly resilient. She maintains a close relationship with her foster family and considers them her family. However, Betsy has also placed significant attention on learning and becoming comfortable in her identity of being an African American woman.

FUNCTION:
Blood is Thick and Forever

Eddy is in his mid thirties. He is college educated and has done well professionally. He has struggled in adult relationships and is currently divorced with two children in the custody of his ex-wife. He prides himself on being a good father and is very proud of his children.

When Eddy was eight, his father shot and killed his mother in a drunken rage. Eddy and his siblings witnessed the murder. They were placed with a relative and spent the next two years being shuffled between various extended family members. Eventually, a relative contacted child welfare services and indicated they could not continue to care for the children.

Eddy entered the child welfare system when he was ten along with his two younger siblings. The children were not able to be placed together and were placed in different foster homes. This was extremely difficult for Eddy and he tried to parent his younger siblings from a distance.

Throughout Eddy's early foster care placements, he often ran away and attempted to reach his siblings. Eventually his running away behavior was judged to be so chronic that he was placed in the juvenile justice system. Eddie was placed in a correctional facility. Following the correctional placement, he was placed in group care for approximately eighteen months.

At age fourteen, Eddy was placed in long term foster care. Accommodations were made for Eddy to have contact with his siblings who were also now in juvenile correctional facilities. Eddy's father was incarcerated in a different State. Eddy was allowed to have regularly scheduled supervised phone contact with his father. His father presented numerous challenges during the phone contacts. He pressured Eddy to parent his siblings and blamed numerous systems for his difficulties and the breakup of his family. Additionally, he would subtlety undermine the foster parents. Eddy would quickly slip into a pattern of advising his father on how to behave on the calls. The calls were important to Eddy, they were also difficult because of his father's pressure to meet his unhealthy expectations.

Eddy remained in the same foster home for four years.

He presented periodic challenges but none that could not be handled by his foster parents. Eddy always appreciated his foster parent's support of him visiting his siblings, and the opening of their home to his siblings on holidays and special occasions.

Eddy's 18th birthday was approximately two months prior to his high school graduation. This was significant for two reasons. The first reason is that all youth in foster care dream of being eighteen because they have wanted for years to be free of system control, foster parents, and social workers. Secondly, Eddy was going to be the first person in his family to ever graduate from high school. Eddy, his foster parents, and I were all excited about this accomplishment. Because of legalities, Eddy was required to sign himself into foster care at eighteen so that he could remain with his foster parents until he graduated from high school. We had discussed the sign-in process many times and Eddy always expressed a desire to do so.

On Eddy's eighteenth birthday, he checked himself out of foster care. He went to the bus depot and bought a ticket to the community where his father was imprisoned.

Eddy avoided contact with me and his foster parents for approximately two years. Eventually he did contact me because of financial needs, but also because he needed to talk about where he wanted to go with his life and where he had been the last two years. As I helped him with a job referral, subsidized housing application, and adult education services, we also talked about his departure at eighteen. Eddy said he needed to make contact with his father for numerous reasons. First of all, he loved his family, inclusive of his father, and he needed to try and understand why he killed his mother, which destroyed their family. His decision didn't have anything to do with him not caring about his foster family. In fact, in hindsight, he regretted hurting them by his early departure from foster care. But Eddy wanted, and always will want, the family into which he was born.

FUNCTION:
Kodak Moments Mean People Care About Me

Heather is a ten year old young lady who has been in eighteen different placements prior to entering treatment foster care. These placements have been a combination of a foster care, emergency shelter care and numerous kinship care placements.

Heather entered treatment foster care with a number of challenges that played-out in the home, school and community. In Heather's nineteenth placement, she was fortunate to be placed with an experienced, caring, treatment foster family; to be case managed by an experienced and involved social worker; and to be placed in a school that was willing to work in a non-traditional manner in responding to the challenges that Heather brought to the school setting. As a result, Heather began to stabilize and respond to multiple, consistent, helping efforts in her life.

As with all youth in foster care, Permanency Planning must plan for the best permanent option for foster youth. In Heather's situation, adoption with an extended family member was the primary permanency goal with a concurrent plan of adoption with a non-family member. An extended family member from a neighboring State did express an interest in adopting Heather. As a result, the custodial agency began the adoptive evaluation process which included visitations. Heather was extremely excited to learn that an extended family member had come forward and expressed an interest in caring for her. The custodial agency did an excellent job in communicating with Heather that this was a possible option for her and that adoption was not a guaranteed outcome. Unfortunately, no matter how carefully and professionally this communication was handled, Heather's interpretation was that a family member wanted her as their own.

Initially the visitations seemed to be going well with Heather and her relatives. Quite suddenly, Heather's extended family withdrew from visiting. They also would not return phone calls to the custodian. Eventually, the custodian was able to make contact with the extended family and they indicated that Heather's challenges were too significant for them and that they were no longer interested in adopting.

The news that Heather's extended family was no longer interested in adopting her was devastating. She quickly regressed behaviorally, and emotionally. Heather's treatment foster family, therapist, social worker, and teachers all tried to support her to the best of his/her ability. However, the reality of losing another potentially permanent family was overwhelming for Heather.

For all of the caring adults in Heather's life, the question quickly became, "How do you support a child that has been repeatedly disappointed by adults?" Heather's treatment team looked at a variety of ways to accomplish this goal. The team had to consider how to support Heather and yet not minimize the painful reality of her situation. The team also had to present the plan in a way that Heather could comprehend and understand.

Heather was provided with a number of disposable cameras. Heather's treatment team encouraged the numerous adults in Heather's life to ask to have their picture taken with her because they enjoyed knowing her and cared about her. The adults made the experience of having the pictures taken a "positive big deal." After the pictures were developed, they were posted on the walls of Heather's room. Additionally, Heather's foster parents bought a large calendar for Heather's room. At bedtime, the foster parents crossed off the day and told Heather that the crossed off day represented another day that Heather was cared about in their family. At the end of the month, the foster family took a very special picture of Heather. In the photo, beside Heather, was the month's calendar with an extra sheet describing all of the things Heather did in that month. The monthly story stressed how much Heather was cared about in her foster family and community. The calendar pages then became a scrapbook.

Heather eagerly involved herself with her cameras. The cameras were fun, they provided Heather with a visual connection to the people that cared about her, and they were displayed in a manner where she was consistently reminded of them. This was not the only intervention that benefited Heather, but it was the intervention that most helped Heather begin to re-establish emotional resilience in relation to some terribly difficult and ongoing disappointments in her life.

FUNCTION:
I Don't Have a Sleep Disorder;
I Just Want to Feel Safe

Carol, age six, was placed in foster care on an emergency basis. As the foster family settled Carol in for her first evening, they showed her the bedroom where she was expected to sleep. Carol reacted very negatively to sleeping in the bedroom. The foster parents backed away from the conflict and told Carol she could sleep wherever she felt comfortable. They provided her with a pillow and blanket and allowed the situation to unfold. Carol decided to sleep in the living room where she could see all of the bedroom doors. Although restless, she was eventually able to go to sleep.

As often happens, little information was known about Carol prior to her entering emergency foster care. As more information became known about Carol's background, it became more apparent why Carol wanted to sleep in the living room and be able to see all the bedroom doors. Carol had been passed among numerous homes in a family system that was highly involved in addiction. Carol's mother was often homeless and on the run. Carol would weekly, and sometimes daily, be sleeping in a place unknown to her. By age six, she had developed the ability to know how to protect herself through restless sleep and physically positioning herself so that she could quickly scan the environment for potential harm. It was a smart adaptation for a six year old in her circumstances.

Carol's emergency placement became a long term foster care placement. Eventually Carol was able to trust the foster home to the point where she was able to sleep in a bedroom. However, what these foster parents wisely identified was that Carol's trusting of their home would be on Carol's time frame, not theirs.

FUNCTION:
I Need to Center Myself Before I Start the Day

Staci is an eleven-year-old young lady who came to treatment foster care after an eighteen month treatment stay in a residential care facility. Prior to being placed in residential care, Staci was in the care of her mother. Staci's mother suffers from a severe mental illness. Unfortunately, Staci had numerous bizarre, abusive, and unpredictable experiences while residing with her mother. The mother's parental rights have been terminated and it is hoped that Staci can be adopted after she is stabilized in treatment foster care.

As with many families, morning is a chaotic time as children ready themselves for school and parents feel rushed to direct a morning routine in a limited time frame. This certainly applies to Staci and her foster family. The foster mother directs the morning routine as the foster father needs to be at work at an earlier time.

Mornings with Staci have become a routine of extreme stress for both the foster mother and Staci. Staci resists getting up in the morning, resists getting dressed, resists taking care of hygiene needs, which results in a breakfast of "pop tarts in the car" and chronic tardiness to work and school. A number of restrictive consequences have been applied to Staci's behavior in the mornings, which have not resulted in any improvements.

The foster parents and their social worker discussed the morning routine in detail. Instead of continuing to look at the morning routine from the perspective of Staci's resistance, they began to look at the morning routine from the perspective of what Staci needs in the morning. They were able to identify that Staci's morning resistance had become a pattern of engagement with the foster mother. They also discovered that before Staci would move forward with any tasks in the morning, she daily needed to locate and play with the family dog. The foster parents noticed that if Staci could play with the family dog prior to other morning tasks, she usually could engage in the tasks in a more cooperative mood. The foster parents also identified that prior to going to bed each night, Staci would bring lotion to her foster parents and ask them to give her a back rub.

As a result of looking at the morning routine from a perspective of what Staci needs in the morning, the foster parents and their social worker designed the following routine. The foster mother began the day by calmly waking Staci and giving her a quick, gentle, backrub. As Staci received her backrub, the foster mother would calmly talk to her in an engaging, supportive way. The foster mother would then invite Staci to join her in the bathroom while the foster mother put on her make-up. The mother had already brought the dog into the bathroom, so that Staci could play with the family dog prior to engaging in her morning tasks.

The foster mother estimates that 85% of the time the new morning routine works. In addition to helping with many mornings, this "new approach" also helped the foster parents and their social worker view Staci's behavior from a functional perspective, which was effective in responding to Staci's challenges in a more supportive and thoughtful manner.

FUNCTION:
I Need to Feel Comfortable in Order to Shower

Roger entered foster care as a result of substantiated sexual abuse at age eight. Behaviorally, Roger is a quiet, compliant young man. However, he was resistant to one area of his care; he refused to take a shower. He would pretend to take a shower by turning on the shower, dampening the wash cloth, soap and towels. Obviously, not showering caused many secondary problems for Roger. The foster parents felt a great deal of pressure to help Roger with his hygiene skills. The foster parents were frustrated over the shower refusal, and then began a cycle of alternating between patience and demanding that Roger follow through with a shower. Neither approach worked, which was even more frustrating.

In response to Roger's shower refusal, the foster parents and their social worker designed a shower routine that was highly sensitive to the issues of sexual abuse. Issues that were highlighted included how to make the bathroom safe, how to respond to the sensory aspects of showering, how to separate showering from sexualized behavior, and rewarding compliance for showering.

The first step in Roger's shower routine included putting a lock on the bathroom door. It was clarified with Roger that there were two keys for the bathroom door, one that would be Roger's and one that would remain with the foster parents. The foster parents clarified that they would not enter the bathroom when Roger was showering. The second step in the plan was that Roger's social worker would show Roger, while both were fully clothed, where it is important to shower as a young man. The third step was that Roger was given a choice in selecting what shower items felt comfortable for him. These items included selecting between bar soap and liquid soap, selecting between washcloths, sponges, or shower puffs and selecting the texture of the towels. Roger was asked if there was anything else that would make him comfortable in the shower. Roger asked if the foster parents would be close to the bathroom when he showered and the foster parents assured him they would be if he would find this supportive, which he did. When Roger successfully showered, the foster parents always positively reinforced his behavior.

Eventually Roger's resistance to showering extinguished, probably as a result of him having established a sense of personal control and feeling comfortable in a situation where he once felt vulnerable.

Chapter Seven

FUNCTION:
I'll Fight So I Can Know My Father

Chad is a ten-year-old young man in foster care. He was removed from the custody of his mother due to her severe mental illness and because she was physically abusive and negligent in her care of him. Parental rights have been terminated on both of Chad's parents. Chad's father was legally identified, but has never had a relationship with Chad. In fact, relatives and friends of Chad's family indicate that his father has disappeared and is presumed dead because of his involvement in drug trafficking.

The foster family that is caring for Chad hopes to adopt him. They have provided excellent care to Chad and have seen him through some very difficult times. Chad is involved in therapy and his foster parents are involved collaterally. With counseling assistance, it seems that Chad has accepted that he will not return to his mother but he clings to a hope that his unknown father will return so that he and Chad can be reunited. In therapy, attention has been placed on the reality of Chad's father with support and understanding for Chad's reunification hopes. Chad reacts angrily when anyone questions, or attempts to present a different perspective regarding his father's intentions. Chad's foster father is especially targeted by Chad's angry feelings. He doesn't want anyone to crush his hopes of reunifying with his birth father.

At times in the foster home, Chad will initiate conversations regarding his father. If these conversations do not go the way Chad hoped, he will quickly escalate and make certain his foster father knows that he isn't his "real" father.

One evening, the foster father suggested that he and Chad write his father a letter. The foster father assured him that the letter would be Chad's thoughts and feelings. The foster father also prepared a box where Chad could store the letters. He encouraged Chad to put items, and additional letters, in the box so that if, or when, Chad's father would contact him, Chad could give him the letters. This way, Chad's birth father would know how often Chad thought about him.

Chad found the "letter box" appealing and calming. It provided him with a symbolic outlet for the grief and pain that he felt by not knowing his father. The partnership of working with his foster father on the letter box validated that Chad's foster father honored his feelings. Additionally, the mutual involvement on the letter box demonstrated that Chad and his foster father could have a relationship that was not threatening to Chad's desire to be with, and know, his birth father.

FUNCTION:
I Need Distance From My Feelings

Lindsey is a thirteen-year-old young lady who is in a foster-adopt placement. Lindsey is a quiet, intense young lady who often seems on the verge of losing her temper. She can easily move into raging although this is slowly improving in her foster-adopt placement.

Lindsey has plenty of valid reasons for being full of rage. Her parents are both chemically dependent and had been extremely abusive to her in the craziness of their chemical dependency. Their parental rights have been terminated because of the severity of the abuse. Lindsey's birth parents used to tie her to her bed when they were gone. She would be tied to the bed for days. Eventually Lindsey learned how to untie herself, meet her own needs in her parent's absence, and re-tie herself before her parents returned to the home.

Lindsey is unable to discuss the abuse she experienced. Her feelings about the abuse often cause her emotional turmoil which she projects onto her foster-adoptive parents. Fortunately Lindsey was referred to a skilled therapist who is knowledgeable about the dynamics of physical abuse and also the dynamics of being in out of home care. The therapist quickly realized the importance of Lindsey being able to "work through" the feelings associated with being a victim of abuse. She also realized the importance of allowing Lindsey to protect herself from the emotional pain of disclosing emotions associated with the abuse. After a number of sessions that focused on establishing a relationship, the therapist asked Lindsey if she would help her with a project. The therapist explained to Lindsey that she counseled a number of youth in foster care and wanted to write a book about what it was like for youth to be in foster care in order to help others in similar situations. The therapist assured Lindsey that it was up to her if she wanted to be part of the book project. With a degree of enthusiasm, Lindsey agreed to assist with the "book project."

The therapist carefully planned the sessions with Lindsey as they worked on the "book project." The therapist positioned herself at her computer and typed Lindsey's story of her experience in foster care. Lindsey answered a number of pre-planned questions prepared by the therapist. After every session, the therapist would edit the material and identify dynamics that were important to positively reinforce with Lindsey. Each new session begins with the therapist reviewing Lindsey's work from the last session. This includes positive reinforcement for the strength that Lindsey displayed in her story shared the previous week. The progression of their work eventually reached the chapters on why youth are placed in foster care. These were very difficult chapters through which Lindsey was able to disclose information on the abuse she experienced. Eventually the book was completed. The therapist entitled the book "Lindsey's Story." She presented the completed book to Lindsey. Surprisingly, Lindsey asked if she could share her story with the potential adoptive parents through some joint sessions.

All of us need to have our "story" validated, accepted and respected by the people that care about us. Unfortunately, stories of abuse can be so painful to disclose that they often remain emotionally internalized and become expressed through rage and other self destructive behaviors. Fortunately, in Lindsey's life, she was able to find an adult, and eventually a family, who were able to provide a safe and caring environment where her story could be told.

FUNCTION:
Help Me Self-Soothe in a Non-sexual Way

Holly is a six-year-old young lady who comes from a family of six. Her father is "on the run" and her mother is unable to care for and protect her children. All of the children were sexually abused by various relatives and "friends of the family."

There are many tragedies associated with the sexual abuse of children. One of the tragedies of sexual abuse is that children are prematurely introduced, in an exploitative manner, to sexual activity that they are not able to understand physically or emotionally. All too often, the victimized child experiences a physical response to the sexual abuse that they adapt to their needs on an emotional and physical level. In Holly's case, she would masturbate to the point where she would cause herself physical injury.

Holly's foster mother is a wonderfully patient person who remains committed to her care but is very concerned about the excessive masturbation. She struggles with how to try to respond and contain the masturbation in a way that is not punitive or shaming. Holly's treatment team identified that the masturbation had become a way for her to self-soothe in a familiar way that caused her to physically calm.

Holly is involved in therapy through a play therapy model. The therapist indicated that Holly involves herself in the therapy but the therapy has not impacted the masturbation. The treatment team struggled with how to respond to the function and purpose of the masturbation in a more appropriate manner.

Eventually the treatment team asked the foster mother to spend time with Holly in a "lotion intervention." While rubbing the lotion on herself the foster mother was asked to talk with Holly about how the lotion smelled good, how the lotion relaxed her and that whenever she was tense or worried she would rub some lotion to calm herself. The foster mother then put some lotion on Holly and slowly rubbed the lotion on her in non-sexualized areas of her body. The foster mother also repeated the messages about how the lotion smelled good and how it was relaxing, especially when a person was tense or worried. She asked Holly if she would use the lotion whenever she felt like touching herself. She went on to explain that the lotion was a positive way to relax and feel calm. The foster mother indicated that she would rub the lotion on Holly when she wanted it. Holly also was given her own container of lotion. The foster mother incorporated the lotion routine into a bedtime ritual for Holly.

All of the members of the treatment team were pleasantly surprised with how quickly and consistently the "lotion intervention" decreased Holly's masturbation. Holly would ask for lotion rubs and self initiated the use of the lotion. In addition to the obvious benefit of providing Holly with a healthier alternative to masturbation, Holly also experienced her foster mother as a caring, calming, non-exploitative caregiver as part of the "lotion intervention." The "lotion intervention" is not a cure-all for the pain of being a victim of sexual abuse. However, in Holly's life, it is a step forward in the healing process.

Conclusion

The emotional and behavioral development of the AFK (Adoptive, Foster, or Kinship) child is not easily understood. Seldom do their problems stand alone. Most often they co-exist with several problematic behaviors. They can hit a family like a ton of bricks. They can create circumstances that result in de-stabilization, disruption and lack of progress. AFK parents are left questioning if they are really making a difference. Progress often seems to be short lived and negatively influenced by situational factors. The AFK child's development is fragile, one that does not respond well to change, as change has often resulted in instability for the child. They can regress behaviorally and emotionally over seemingly insignificant experiences.

However, regression does not mean failure. It does mean that the AFK child has experienced a stressor that has destabilized them. So the message to the AFK parent is "steady on the stern." If you succeed in understanding the purposes of the child's behavior and have influenced that behavior through the healing power of a healthy parental relationship that respects the child's context, chances are that the child can heal.

There are some children, in our professional experience, who could not be cared for in an Adoptive, Foster, or Kinship home, but those children are the exception, not the rule. Our respect for the efforts of AFK children, and the families that care for them, can never be fully communicated. Our hope is that "Behavior with a Purpose" illustrates that there is always hope for healing, even when faced with the most traumatic and overwhelming circumstances.

The purpose of understanding
*   is to create optimism, wisdom, and change.*

About our Authors

 **Dr. Rick Delaney** is a nationally known speaker and consultant to foster, kinship, and adoptive parents. He is the clinical director of a community-based residential treatment center for emotionally disturbed children in Kailua-Kona, Hawaii. For many years, Dr. Delaney has been a consultant to the Casey Family Programs and other foster care and adoption agencies across the county. He is the author or co-author of several books in the area of foster care and adoption, including Fostering Changes: Myth, Meaning, and Magic Bullets in Attachment Theory and Troubled Transplants: Unconventional Strategies for Helping Troubled Foster and Adopted Children. He is the principal investigator of Foster Parent College (www.fosterparentcollege.com), an on-line resource for foster and adoptive parents. He has helped to develop an on-line training series for Portland State University's adoption-competent mental health certificate program. Dr. Delaney is a father, step-father and grandfather and lives in Kailua-Kona, Hawaii.

Charley Joyce, LICSW, has been a social worker for 34 years. He began his career as a VISTA volunteer and has worked as the clinical director of a psychiatric facility, as an outpatient therapist, supervisor of outpatient therapists, as a foster care caseworker, as a supervisor and clinical director of treatment foster care services. He is currently employed as a supervisor for PATH, ND Inc. He teaches part-time in the Master of Social Work Program at the University of North Dakota, on-line through the Foster Parent College, Eugene, Oregon and is a contributor for www.toolboxparent.com. Annually he provides numerous trainings for foster-adopt parents and child welfare workers. His MSW is from the University of Iowa and he has completed post-graduate education in family therapy. He has been married to the same person for 34 years and they have two adult daughters.

Index

Abuse 1, 6, 17, 25, 35, 51-52, 55, 67, 87, 92, 95, 107, 117, 127, 130, 131, 143-144, 147-150
Attention Deficit
    ADD 19, 39, 87, 107, 116, 128
    ADHD 12, 87, 107-108, 116, 128
Adjustment Disorders 68
Adoption 120, 138, 153
Adoptive 6, 15, 18, 29, 31, 36, 38, 42, 45, 50, 54, 72-73, 75, 84, 91, 96, 98, 106, 118-120, 138, 148, 151-153
AFK Children 8, 13, 15, 29-31, 37, 57, 73-75, 80, 123, 152
AFK Parent 15, 16, 57, 62, 70, 99, 103, 105-106, 110, 113-116, 118, 124, 126, 128, 151
AFK Youth 14-16, 33, 43, 66-67, 87-90, 96, 98, 101, 109-110, 115-117, 127, 129-130
Anorexia Nervosa 44
Bulimia 45
Child Development 35
Conduct Disorder 5, 87
Defiance 6, 16-17, 91-99, 101-111, 113-117, 132

Depression 7, 44, 47, 96, 102, 115-116
Differential Diagnosis 44, 68, 87, 115, 127
Disruptive Behavior Disorder 68, 116
Feeding Disorder of Infancy or Early Childhood 44
Fetal Alcohol Spectrum Disorders (FASD) 12, 87
Foster Care 6, 15, 18, 20, 24-25, 29-30, 36-37, 43, 45, 51, 60, 62, 64, 75, 93-94, 99, 102, 106, 111-112, 130-132, 135-138, 140-143, 145, 148, 153-154
Hoarding Food 6, 16, 34, 36, 39-40, 42
Kinship 6, 15, 18, 29, 31, 36, 38, 42, 45, 50, 54, 72-73, 75, 84, 91, 96, 98, 106, 118-120, 138, 148, 151-153
Lying 6, 9, 12, 14, 16, 28, 72-74, 80-90, 121
Manipulation 29, 92
Masturbation 149-150
Mood Disorder 68, 115

Negative Attention-Seeking
    Disorder 10, 17, 39, 77, 83,
    85, 119, 121-128
Neglect 6, 16, 24, 35-36, 38-39,
    42-43, 47, 60, 64-67, 69, 74,
    76, 78, 92, 96, 112, 117, 127
Oppositional Defiant Disorder
    (ODD) 22, 115-116, 128
Phobia 11, 77, 84, 121
Pica 44
Post Traumatic Stress Disorder
    (PTSD) 5, 68
Reactive Attachment Disorder
    (RAD) 5, 45, 68-69
Rumination Disorder 44
Self-esteem 6, 7, 86, 92
Self-Parented Child 111, 113-116
Sexualized Behavior 6, 28, 144,
    150
Sleep Disturbance 96
Stealing 6, 16, 28, 29, 38-39,
    72-79, 81, 87, 89-90, 120, 132
Toileting 63-67, 69, 71
Wetting 16, 22, 28, 50-71